MORE
THAN A
SECRET

MORE THAN A SECRET

How a Mistress Broke Free From Her Affair

ALICIA BARR

RESOLVE EDITIONS

More Than a Secret: How a Mistress Broke Free from Her Affair
Copyright © 2026 by Alicia Barr

All rights reserved. No part of this publication may be reproduced, stored in a retrieval system, or transmitted in any form by any means, electronic, mechanical, photocopy, recording, or otherwise, without the prior permission of the publisher, except as provided by USA copyright law.

No patent liability is assumed with respect to the use of the information contained herein. Although every precaution has been taken in the preparation of this book, the publisher and author assume no responsibility for errors or omissions. Neither is any liability assumed for damages resulting from the use of the information contained herein.

Names and identifying details have been changed.

Scripture quotations marked ESV are from the ESV® Bible (The Holy Bible, English Standard Version®), copyright ©2001 by Crossway, a publishing ministry of Good News Publishers. Used by permission. All rights reserved.

Scripture quotations marked NIV are from the Holy Bible, New International Version®, NIV®, Copyright © 1973, 1978, 1984, 2011 by Biblica, Inc.™ Used by permission of Zondervan. All rights reserved worldwide.

Scripture quotations marked NLT are from the Holy Bible, New Living Translation, copyright ©1996, 2004, 2015 by Tyndale House Foundation. Used by permission of Tyndale House Publishers, a Division of Tyndale House Ministries, Carol Stream, Illinois 60188. All rights reserved.

Published by Forefront Books, Nashville, Tennessee.
Distributed by Simon & Schuster.

Library of Congress Control Number: 2025924222

Print ISBN: 978-1-63763-500-1
E-book ISBN: 978-1-63763-501-8

Cover Design by Brad Imburgia, Ember Brand Co.
Interior Design by Mary Susan Oleson, Blu Design Concepts

Printed in the United States of America
26 27 28 29 30 31 RR4 10 9 8 7 6 5 4 3 2 1

To the woman I used to be

COWBOY'S LIE

In the still dark of the morning,

I'd wake up with a smile

to the sound of boots coming my way.

Coffee and comfort waiting at my door.

Lord, how could something so wrong feel so right?

You loved me and left me for another day.

You took me to the moon

and showed me all the stars.

Told me I was the best you'd ever had,

your once-in-a-lifetime love.

You weren't out to hurt the others,

just give you a little more time.

Take the good with the bad

was the anthem I despised.

Four years later, I wake

to the tears rolling down my face.

The pain so great, to die would be gain.

Jesus said, joy comes in the morning.

That's the evil of this secret,

it was never meant to be this way.

Forgiveness, grace, and freedom await.

You took me to the moon

and showed me all the stars.

Told me I was the best you'd ever had,

your once-in-a-lifetime love.

You weren't out to hurt the others,

just give you a little more time.

Take the good with the bad

was the anthem I despised.

Cowboys lie and cowboys cry.

There ain't a tear you shed that I haven't already cried.

My greatest weakness and hardest goodbye,

this is for all the women wanting to die.

CONTENTS

Foreword by Rachel Long 11

Preface.. 13

1. Picture Perfect..................................... 17
2. Cloud Nine 33
3. Tempered Glass 45
4. The Awakening 55
5. Secret Reality..................................... 73
6. Don't Have Secrets............................. 97
7. Amputation 107
8. The Legend...................................... 121
9. Courage to Heal 139
10. Facing My Giants 145
11. The Final Goodbye 161
12. Post-War 189

Appendix: Poems and Reflections 199
Resources 213
About the Author................................. 215
Notes 217
Acknowledgments................................ 219

FOREWORD

Every so often, a story lands in your hands that doesn't just ask to be read—it asks to be felt. *More Than a Secret* is one of those stories.

As a grief counselor and pastor, I've sat with people in the aftermath of loss, betrayal, moral failure, heartbreak, and silence. I've heard the words they don't say out loud. And I've seen how the human heart can survive things we're told should destroy us.

That's why this book matters so much.

The woman who wrote these words does not claim to be a hero. She doesn't pretend to have it all figured out. She shares her truth with a kind of unapologetic vulnerability that is rare and courageous. What you'll find here isn't filtered or polished; it's real. It's the voice of someone willing to walk through the fire and still choose integrity, even if she had to learn it the hard way.

This book will stir up something inside you. It might

FOREWORD

make you uncomfortable. It might make you cry. I believe it will also invite you to ask some powerful questions of your own—about honesty, about relationships, about faith and failure, about what we do when life turns out differently than we hope, and about how we begin again.

If, by chance or divine intervention, you are that woman—the one in the affair, the one who never imagined you'd end up where you are, who feels torn between conviction and connection, the one who feels completely in love and completely lost—this book is especially for you. There are few resources (if any) written with your heartache, hope, and healing in mind. Fewer still that offer compassion without condoning and clarity without condemnation. This story does both. It will not excuse you, but it will see you.

So whether you're flipping these pages out of curiosity, pain, or something you can't yet name, I hope you'll read with an open heart. And maybe, just maybe, this story will help you feel a little less alone in your own sin and struggles.

Pastor Rachel Long, MS,GC-C, CGC
Doctoral Candidate – Human Services 2026
Founder of Joshua Center

PREFACE

How can the best thing in your life make you wish your life would end, abruptly?

I am writing this book to the woman I used to be. It is a story of a relationship where, for the first time in my life, I felt love, passion, and intimacy. It was addicting, exhilarating, and fun—until it wasn't. As you will discover, it is a story of how I fell into an affair with a married man thirty years older than me and *loved it*. I was married at the time as well, *and* I was the happy mistress. However, what started out as so unexpectedly shocking and uplifting morphed into something else over time, something toxic and damaging.

In the pages to come, I'm going to tell you the story of my life, particularly honing in on the last decade, with a level of vulnerability perhaps beyond any book you've ever read. It is the second most courageous, difficult, and painful thing I've ever done to

PREFACE

recount this story, write it, and share it with the world. The first was and is living it.

You will be tempted to perceive me as a victim. Please do not. I take full responsibility for the choices I have made, the sin I embraced, and the actions I have taken. Though I have changed the names of many people involved, I will be real, raw, and genuine with the good, bad, and ugly, because anything less would be a lie, and I've learned the hard way that there is nothing more important to me than my integrity. In fact, I opted to hybrid publish this book so I could give you the real and unfiltered version as I believe that will be the most relatable to every woman who has walked in my shoes or perhaps still is.

Being a secret was never in God's design for humanity. He created boundaries for our relationships to protect us and empower us to experience his gift of intimacy as a blessing, never a curse. What I did was not only wrong but destructive. It nearly killed me. Letting go of the man you will get to know in the pages to come has been the hardest and most painful journey I have ever embarked on.

When I hit rock bottom, amid all the turmoil, I

PREFACE

desperately went searching for someone—anyone—to relate to but came up short. There was not a book, podcast, or any other resource to be found in confidence that would help me make sense of this nightmare I had entered, let alone how to chart a path out of it coming from the mistress's point of view. I wanted nothing more than for God to take me to my final resting place; there was no desirable solution, and the future looked very bleak. My hope and prayer is that this book will be the resource of hope, inspiration, and encouragement that I couldn't find when I needed it most.

> **BEING A SECRET WAS NEVER IN GOD'S DESIGN FOR HUMANITY.**

Should you give this story a chance, I trust you will find the inspiration to not only survive breaking free from the toxicity of an extramarital affair but have the hope of thriving again, living your best and most abundant life in the years to come.

PREFACE

Girl,

You are fearfully and wonderfully made.

You were not made to be anyone's number two.

You are worth more than a secret.

May you find the courage to choose the harder right,

to be the best version of you that you can be.

CHAPTER 1

PICTURE PERFECT

"I'd never cheat, an' I would never lie,
in another's eyes, yeah yeah"

— "In Another's Eyes,"
BY TRISHA YEARWOOD AND GARTH BROOKS

I USED TO tell people I had it made. Raised in small town USA, there was plenty to be grateful for. I grew up in a two-story farmhouse covered in clay-colored vinyl siding and a driftwood-shingled roof on the edge of town with about fourteen acres, a few cows, chickens, an occasional pig or two, usually a dog and/or barn cats, and too many unwelcome coons and possums. Our property had a creek that ran through it, and on the other side, my grandparents, better known as Nana and Papaw, had about forty-four acres of tillable ground and woodland that adjoined. Not even a half mile from our house was their farmhouse on a couple of acres, and on the north end of their farm is the place I grew up visiting every time we wanted to go fishing. Now that is where I live, next to the fishing hole. My parents own the land adjoining, so our properties connect through the field.

I have an amazing younger sister, Ashley, who's always been one of my greatest cheerleaders. Every time I start to question whether a house will sell, a project will get finished, or if I'll ever marry again, I can hear the echo of her voice: "It will," or "You will get it," and "You will." I have some of the hardest-working and most loving parents a kid could ask for who never let us want for anything we ever *needed*. I never got the deck and private entrance I wanted in high school, but the Airbnb guests enjoy it now! Bless their hearts.

I grew up on God, Garth, and Strait. Our house was built on the foundation of faith. We lived a simple life, with a "work hard, play hard" mindset, although work often felt like playing around the farm and we loved it. Going out to eat on a Sunday was a treat, and every meal

PICTURE PERFECT

at my nana and papaw's was heaven on earth, especially when there was a hot apple pie coming out of the oven with a cup of black coffee and vanilla-bean ice cream. I wonder if that's part of God's grand design, the cycle of life, because Lord knows if Nana was still here and I still ate like I did growing up, multiplied by slower metabolism, I'd be in a world of hurt!

A tomboy to the bone, I was confident I could do anything any boy could do and welcomed the challenge. I was my dad and papaw's shadow growing up, learning how to work around the farm, remodel houses, and back trailers before I was tall enough to see over the steering wheel. I grew up with a love for raising cattle while my sister enjoyed horses, perhaps primarily because I could make money selling beef and I hadn't figured out how to turn a dime with a horse. In fact, they seemingly just cost money—hay burners.

When I turned sixteen and got my license, I decided it was time to quit playing sports and start my career. I started "trashing out" (removing what remained from repossessed homes the banks took over) and mowing bank-owned properties for cash flow. My mom was a real estate agent and made the connections for me. This income allowed me to make the down payment and secure my first house, which I later sold for a profit.

At seventeen, I bought my second home and remodeled it during nights and weekends around school. That, too, sold for a profit.

I also borrowed $35,000 to buy thirty-five steers from a Texas ranch. My plan was to supply beef to an all-natural grocery store in Minnesota until nine of the steers died in the first few months—but that's a story for another time, a very painful lesson learned. I worked around the clock to get the loan paid back. Thanks to Dave Ramsey (a personal finance guru I follow) and Proverbs 22:7 ("The rich rule over the poor, and the borrower is slave to the lender," NIV), other than a conservative note on my home for a brief time, I have never gone into debt since. I've never had a credit card, a car loan, or a credit score. Take a breath—I am okay.

Terri Clark's song "One of the Guys" was my anthem, and I took pride in every beat. I never cared much about school and really didn't want to go to college, but my parents thought it would be a good idea to have a "backup." Reluctantly, I agreed to get an associate's degree in business from our state's community college, cramming every class into one day a week so I could work the rest of the week. Yes, yes, I see you, Sabbath; I'm a work in progress. Note to self: I know my parents' motives were well intended, but learning from professors who have never been in business is a waste of time and money. Let's face it, at eighteen years old, what do you have to lose? Go big or go home. And if you go big, be prepared to work harder and longer than all your friends combined—or at least smarter!

Here's what you do in small-town USA: Graduate high school, maybe go to college, maybe not, get married, buy a house, and possibly start a family. I've always been in a hurry, echoing Alabama's song, "I'm in a Hurry (And Don't Know Why)," in real time. I'm known for running a hundred miles an hour in life and business. Living the American dream was no different. I dated a guy named Dan for three years, went through an enormous amount of church classes and counseling, tied the knot, and bought the house by the fishing hole about a half mile from where I grew up. I had no complaints.

I was following the formula I learned, going through the motions, climbing my own entrepreneurial ladder, heavily involved in church and small groups, family, and maintaining our slice of paradise surrounded by corn and beans. I was full of life, confident, strong, and successful for my age by most definitions. I had everything going for me and never shied away from hard work or hard times. I learned early on to press in, and when the going got tough, I got tougher.

Sometimes you simply don't know what you don't know. I was naïve and young, striving to be a sponge and soak every bit of knowledge and wisdom up, whether personally or professionally. I was content. I really didn't know anything better to stack my life up against in this little town. I was a virgin when I married, and when I finally had sex on my wedding night, I had to wonder what all the hype was about. I went through the motions, focused on work, family, church, Jesus, and being the best version of me I could be on this journey called life.

It's important for you to know and be mindful of where I come from and who I was growing up as you continue to read and digest the unfolding story with all of life's turns and fast curveballs. I was a God-fearing, Jesus-loving farm girl high on country living from small town USA. I was predictable, dependable, and loyal to a fault.

PICTURE PERFECT

An overachiever, of whom nobody would have higher expectations than myself. A young go-getter, determined to work harder and longer than anyone and everyone around me, to experience a life that generations prior only dreamed of. A girl who saw the straight and narrow as the only path if she didn't want God's wrath. A warrior of sorts, a phone call away for her family, friends, and neighbors. Always eager to help, serve, and inspire to greater heights. A good human by every standard, though far from perfect. I put an excessive amount of pressure on myself. I was confident but also judgmental, although most would never know. I struggled with control, even with my Maker: *Why couldn't things be the way I thought they should be?*

When I was eighteen years old, my family met some folks, whom I am calling John-Boy and Jenni, and who became near and dear to our hearts. In fact, they grew to be more like family than friends. The first point of connection was probably how we dressed: more often than not, jeans, boots, and a casual shirt. We were all from small country towns, high on country living, country music, and hard work.

John-Boy became like a big brother to me, and let me tell you, there is only one John-Boy in this world, so unique, always making me laugh, and always "good"—no matter the circumstances. Jenni was a lot of fun too. Running with the kids, sharing meals, going to concerts, we shared a lot of laughs and hazelnut coffee. We loved their kids like they were our own, eager to help with schoolwork, play, bake, attend rodeos, or any other fun we could find.

SOMETIMES YOU SIMPLY DON'T KNOW WHAT YOU DON'T KNOW.

John-Boy and Jenni were not locals but had been here some time. At one point, they moved back to their home state and sold their nearby home. When they decided to move back and plant roots here, they were trying to figure out what that would look like. In the meantime, they had rented a couple of different farms that weren't shaking out like expected. My husband and I were talking more and more about how we could support them in their endeavors. John-Boy and Jenni were both in our wedding, and I don't think there was anything we

PICTURE PERFECT

wouldn't do for them.

The idea arose for them to build a boarding facility for horses on our property with living quarters above it, which would be only three and a half miles from the horse track. We started checking into what that would entail, made the plans, counted the cost, sought the county's blessing, and we were off!

For six months John-Boy and Jenni lived in my parents' upper-level, half a mile from Dan's and my place while we constructed the new three-thousand-square-foot barn. The barn would be equipped with ten horse stalls, five on each side and an open center to store hay and still have a walking path for the horses. There would be a wash bay, a half bath, and a tack room extending out the front of the building on the main level. Above that enclosed space was a massive twelve-by-thirty-foot deck leading into a rustic nine hundred square feet of living quarters. It would be perfect for them, and even easier for all of us to do life together only 150 yards away from Dan's and my home.

I had spent the last few years relentlessly reading, learning, and attending as many Dave Ramsey live events as I could. One of his key speakers and leaders I had grown to respect had since resigned and started facilitating life-changing events, what was then known as "Life Plan," for anyone who was interested. Life Plan was an intensive one-on-one coaching event to help you lay out your life on the whiteboard, understand what caused the greatest falls and what inspired the biggest leaps, in an effort to live your best life moving forward. It was a two-day commitment on the outskirts of Nashville, and I jumped at the opportunity to sign up and go.

I loved it! It challenged me to look in the rearview mirror long enough to discover and see the patterns in my life and what caused various painful falls. These insights and lessons helped me form a vision for my future. I've always been intrigued by the self-help world, learning how to get, and be, better. I came back from Nashville so excited that I encouraged everyone in my circle to go through the program. Ultimately, at various times, my parents, sister, aunt, and even John-Boy went through it.

John-Boy called me at the conclusion of his first day. I could hear the excitement in his voice. I was excited for him and couldn't wait for Jenni to go. The program brought so much clarity, healing, and hope for each of us

PICTURE PERFECT

to discover and embrace. We all have something special inside, right? Because of the program, how I saw others changed. My level of empathy grew. I learned that no parent gets it perfect, no child grows up flawless. Now, thanks to Life Plan, every time I cross paths with someone with a less-than-kind interaction, I think to myself, *She's just a broken-hearted little girl in a woman's body* or *He's just a broken-hearted little boy in a man's body.* For every human, I became innately aware that "hurt people hurt people."

John-Boy and Jenni had truly become like family. When they moved in upon completion of the living quarters, Dan and I, my parents, and my aunt continued to rotate houses with them for dinner multiple times a week and were getting to know one another even better—the good, the bad, and the ugly.

I was excited.

Jenni had agreed to go to Life Plan, but within days of her departure date, she not only bowed out but deflected by running to the church I had attended for nearly twenty years, creating a huge monster over John-Boy's and my friendship. I guess looking in the mirror was too daunting.

I was not too worried. I had not only attended this church for twenty years but had served alongside their leadership, leading and participating in several programs and ministries. They knew me.

What happened next shocked and wrecked me. Rather than offering accountability and attempting to get to the root of the deflection and dysfunction, the church simply sided with Jenni, coddling her while castrating John-Boy. My heart ached. All along I had wanted for my friends to find healing from their past, hope for their future, and to begin to thrive in their marriage and in life. Instead, the church was enabling Jenni's fears and failing the couple and their family right before my eyes.

Eventually, the senior pastor met with me and Dan. I asked him, "Do you believe the definition of insanity, doing the same thing over and over and expecting different results?"

"No, not entirely," the pastor responded.

This is what I saw the church doing for Jenni, the same thing they had done again and again, instructing Jenni to meet with a volunteer counselor, read a book, and participate in a small group. This prescription had not helped Jenni get to the root of her pain or find healing.

PICTURE PERFECT

What made them think the same prescription would produce a different result this time? Within six months of moving into the new barn and home, John-Boy and Jenni moved out.

I was devastated. While I could not conceive of having a romantic relationship with John-Boy, he was nevertheless my best friend, my "adopted" older brother. We had so many common interests. Life was fun with John-Boy and Jenni and their kids.

Dan voiced his support for me, even for John-Boy and my friendship. He told the church he didn't have any concern or fear whatsoever. But it made no difference. Unfortunately, without any support, John-Boy bowed down and bowed out, going along with everything Jenni and the church ordered.

Is it possible that his and my friendship was stronger than their marriage? Maybe so. But I did not know that, and I could not see how anything I had done could be construed as wrong or inappropriate. My heart was in shreds.

Although the senior pastor apologized for "failing us" in this situation, he was not willing to "right the wrong." My parents, Dan, and I decided to leave that church. We could not, in good conscience, continue to support a church that took the easy way out rather than pursuing the "harder right" (which is my shorthand for doing the harder but right thing). Jesus never did. It all seemed very unfortunate and unnecessary. Where would we go to worship? What would life be like without the closest friends we'd ever had?

And what, on God's green earth, would we do with this massive reminder in our backyard? This three-thousand-square-foot horse barn stood nearly thirty feet high with living quarters and no horses or people and was situated at the backdrop of our pond. With every sunset it was a reminder of the failed friendships and venture. To say I felt disappointed and sad was an understatement.

But I am not one to mope. I am a doer by nature and so those emotions rolled into a momentous attempt at redemption. A year later, when horse-racing season was firing up yet again, and only being three miles from a major racetrack, I posted some flyers and let people know we had a horse barn for rent. I attended association meetings and started making calls.

I reached out to a reputable outfit and got an initial "No thanks." But a few days later he called back and said

PICTURE PERFECT

he and his wife would like to come and see the place. I made sure the barn looked its best: lights on, mats swept, shedrow raked, wash bay rinsed. It was show ready. After all, your first impression is your last impression.

CHAPTER 2

CLOUD NINE

It was a clear, sunny day, and I was excited at the prospect of the barn being filled with horses again, not to mention recouping some of the money Dan and I had spent on this failed endeavor. A couple pulled up in a small, clean, and crisp SUV. I welcomed them with a firm handshake and bright smile—yes sir, yes ma'am, just the way I was raised. A clean-cut, well-dressed, classy couple whom I estimated to be a little older than my parents, Mav and Mary were kind and seemed impressed other than the stalls being a little smaller than Mav preferred. A short time later, Mav called to confirm they wanted to rent the facility.

I was twenty-seven years old, full of life, energy, and

fire. When they called or texted with any request, I was on it or had someone on it. In fact, a few days after the horses moved in, Mav called and said one of the horses had chewed on the bubble-wrap wall insulation just outside the stall gate. He apologized and asked if maybe when my husband got home, he could put some plywood up. He didn't know me yet—I had both walls protected before my husband ever left work.

Mav noticed, and with a grin said, "You did that, didn't you?"

"Yes," I replied. I had been around construction my whole life. I had been taught by men, but I no longer needed men to get a simple job done. There was a full-time groom responsible for feeding, grooming, and exercising the horses as well as cleaning the stalls. The groom stayed at the barn to tend to the horses, but Mav and Mary would still pop in and out frequently.

Upon learning that I bought, remodeled, and sold houses for a living, they shared that they were in the midst of building their own barn a few miles down the road and didn't have a lot of connections here yet. They welcomed Dan and me with open arms, and the next thing I knew, I was amped to be helping with the construction and

CLOUD NINE

completion of their barn and living quarters. Mary and I would run to the store, picking out and picking up material and supplies. We were very different in so many ways but similar in others. She always looked the part, with her nails, makeup, and hair intact, while I, on the other hand, lived in a man's world and wasn't ever too concerned about my outward appearance. We got along well, sharing a love for coffee, kids, beaches, good food, and good times. Now she had an accomplice to give Mav a taste of his own sarcasm.

Construction wasn't Mav's jam at all. He would occasionally come to harass us for a minute and reluctantly help, but usually he found a task that he "had" to complete revolving around the horses, pasture, or his dog. Although he and I didn't share our love for coffee or dogs, we were both fierce competitors and die-hard entrepreneurs. We were a match in our determination, work ethic, and will to win.

Mav and I had a few starkly different preferences on nonessentials but paralleled stronger than anyone I had ever known on the essentials. Work, winning, and having fun along the way fueled us in a way that I would venture to guess few have ever experienced. Mav was a man of few words in public. But whether it was going down the road or working at the farm, there did not seem to be enough time to hear all the stories, learn all the intricacies of why he did what he did, or how he navigated life, business, and success. I had an unceasing desire for more time, to just learn and listen. This was perplexing for a gal who had always done most of the talking.

I'll never forget one day early on, I was at their property, and Mav and Mary already had some horses in the small fields, or paddocks, out back. They asked me to go back there with them, never bothering to tell me they needed extra hands to hold horses they were going to catch. Mind you, I never really took interest in horses growing up, only cattle. So it had been years since I'd held a horse, let alone a racehorse.

I remarked, "I don't handle horses. I don't know what I'm doing."

The next thing I knew there was a lead rope attached to a halter on a horse in my hand. They laughed, with me joining in nervously, spazzed out and rolling with it. Thankfully, nobody got hurt from my ignorance! That was the first lead rope I would hold of thousands over the next few years.

CLOUD NINE

Dan and I began attending a race here and there—then every race, it seemed. I was fascinated. I hadn't been around any sports competition since playing basketball in high school. Dan and I started having conversations about buying a racehorse or partnering with Mav and Mary. Six months later, we were taking trips to look at potential horses, laughing and cutting up most of the way, as I recall. It wasn't long before we had bought into not just one but a few racehorses after being told distinctly, "You will have eleven chances to lose in every twelve-horse race."

Sounds like fun! I thought. Sometimes I wonder if I had "Stupid" written on my forehead! I was getting into a business I knew nothing about, and I had never been so excited.

Have you ever been inspired, energized, and empowered by something unexpected? It was like a piece of me came to life that I never knew existed. I didn't know I had been missing anything until I realized what I now had. A new fire had been lit within me, sparking excitement, joy, laughter, and adrenaline in a field and with people I had only known for a few fast months. It was a fire that displaced the logic and sense I had leaned on my whole life.

MORE THAN A SECRET

I WAS GETTING INTO A BUSINESS I KNEW NOTHING ABOUT, AND I HAD NEVER BEEN SO EXCITED.

In exchange for Mav's team training our horses, I started helping with the horses, primarily hauling them in and out of the track. Meanwhile, I assisted with finishing the living quarters at their new facility and helping with anything and everything I could around the farm. Mav worked with several full-time grooms, but he or I always watered and worked the track every day, pushed up and/or loaded manure to be hauled away, sometimes hauling it away ourselves. Anything that broke was fixed by one or both of us. All the horses out back had automatic waterers, but we threw grain twice a day and had to keep hay out in each of the paddocks. If it was a race day, after hauling between the farm and the track, I'd often go back to the track to help hand-walk the horses that were racing that day or haul hay and feed to the track, or both. Some days a semi load of large rectangular hay bales would roll

CLOUD NINE

in at the farm to unload with the tractor, and other days we'd be going to pick up loads of small square bales of hay. Many days consisted of one or both of us making runs to a vet clinic. There was always something, and I was always ready to do what I could to lighten Mav's load.

Soon, construction of Mav and Mary's facility was complete. While we all had been working together on the barn and apartment and growing friendships practically around the clock for six months, now it was often just Mav and me. Mary primarily took care of paperwork while my husband worked a full-time job. We each carried on with our respective businesses while also working with each other every day and talking fifteen times a day. I would cross paths with Mary at the farm when I pulled in to swap horses and oftentimes in the chaos of training hours at the track, but we didn't have nearly the time as we did prior to the racing season starting. The four of us would all gather at race time and usually grab a bite to eat afterward or, at minimum, a drink to celebrate.

Although we didn't win every race, we won *a lot*, and I was having the time of my life. For the first time in over a decade, I felt like an intricate part of a winning team, and the team captain had all the confidence in the world in me. Work felt like play—even pushing up and loading manure on the open station tractor. The sawdust particles would fly like snow and make me reek of the smell for the rest of the day, but it didn't faze me. I never dreaded a day or a task and always woke up before my alarm, eager to get the day going.

Mav handed me more and more responsibility and sincerely believed I could do anything I put my mind to, entrusting me with his most valuable assets and deepest secrets. We shared an ever growing and evolving respect for each other both professionally and personally. He said he had been around very few women in his life that had a natural bent with the racehorses. He had me hauling across state lines solo in no time and never hesitated to roll the dice with me. One time, he, Mary, and I traveled to another state for a race, and he didn't have anyone to take the horse up for the race. Guess who got a groom's license in that state in the blink of an eye? Yeah, he was great at getting me out of my comfort zone, without even asking!

We became so comfortable in each other's world that we talked about anything and everything. Mav began voicing that his wife was getting jealous of my presence, although she was never transparent with me about that,

CLOUD NINE

despite my efforts to proactively resolve any issues. It was just over a year after we had met, six months after finishing the barn, when his phone rang. I could hear Mary screaming at him. I had gone along with him to the vet's clinic like we had done so many times, but clearly, it wasn't as well received as it had been before. I was beside myself. This was a couple twice my age, and a wife so jealous she couldn't keep her composure. I was devastated. I never, ever saw this coming—*again*.

What was it about me causing these women to feel threatened, intimidated, or envious? I thought, *I am confident, and I am kind. I am attractive, but so are they. I am supportive, respectful, encouraging, not just of their husbands, but of them. I have served them and their families in ways most people wouldn't comprehend doing on their own time and dollar. I'm not intimidating, but they are intimidated—why? What have they experienced that they are so fearful of the platonic friendship their husbands and I share? These wives have platonic friendships themselves that never seemed to be problematic. Why does the fact that I've always been a guy's gal feel like a curse in my life now?*

I felt doomed. My hope of ever enjoying a thriving platonic friendship without hindering another relationship was fading fast. John-Boy had been like an older brother—fourteen years older to be exact. Mav, on the other hand, was thirty years older than me. Yet, it made no difference. Both spouses grew to envy me. Both Jenni and Mary became consumed with jealousy.

The biggest difference between John-Boy and Mav, though, was their personalities. John-Boy, like my husband and my dad, had a passive personality and ran from conflict. Mav, on the other hand, had a dominant personality and was not scared of conflict. He would do what he felt was best, period. And he felt it best for me to be around and help with the operations I had become so intricately involved with. I had never experienced someone so ready and willing to fight for me, perhaps because nobody had ever needed to. I felt wanted, valued, and safe.

Mav was unique to me, the first man I'd ever personally known who actually called the shots day in and day out. He led his wife, family, house, team, and business. It was different, but a good different. He wasn't arrogant about it. In fact, he offered a tremendous amount of respect for those he cared for the most and carefully considered what they thought. I trusted him with every fiber of my being. So rather than cause the control freak in me to flip out for being out of control, I found peace and confidence in being led by him, not only in our joint efforts with work, but in life. It was like a weight lifted from my shoulders, and I hadn't even really known a weight existed at the time.

Mav had lived a lot more life than me, and naturally I felt there was much wisdom to glean from him. Despite not understanding or agreeing with every decision he made, I never hesitated to follow him. I recall sharing with him that my sister had jokingly commented, "You will never be able to work for someone else."

He looked at me, perplexed. I explained with a chuckle, "You know, I'm so independent, controlling, and decisive; she doesn't see me taking orders from anyone else."

He replied, "We've never had a problem since you've been helping me."

True, I thought to myself, with an epiphany of revelation. Heck, I've had people suggest I will struggle to be in a relationship because of my independence and dominant personality. Yet, thanks to my time with Mav, I know that with the right man, a man that I fully trust and respect, a man that reciprocates trust and respect, being led will be a relief, not a burden.

I can remember sitting on the black fender of an old flatbed bumper-pull trailer as he sat on the fender across from me. We had picked up some heavy one-inch rubber belting that would eventually be used to line one side of the horse trailer floor to ease his OCD over the horses "pawing" a hole in the floor every time the trailer came to a stop. We went to the back forty and backed it up near a tree line, dropped the ramp, and dragged the belting off with channel locks. He could see the weight and fear in my eyes, having just lost one of the closest friends I'd ever had two years prior, to an insecure and jealous wife.

I asked, "What are we going to do? We both know Mary's got a major problem with me, and we have all these horses together."

He responded definitively, without hesitation, "Don't you worry, there will be a divorce before we liquidate horses."

CHAPTER 3

TEMPERED GLASS

IMAGINE DROPPING a picture-perfect portrait. Not the one that has glass that shatters into a million pieces and scatters everywhere, but the one that is protected by tempered glass, like mine. It cracks, creaks, and shatters slowly, often holding together despite there being a million little lines in countless directions. You can't see the picture anymore for the shattered glass still covering it.

In my life, there was a lot going on behind that glass and I wasn't the least bit mad about it.

My husband, Dan, and I had been trying to start a family the year prior to meeting Mav and Mary, but to no avail. While I absolutely love and adore kids, I could not and still can't imagine being pregnant or having kids.

My second home consists of crawl spaces and attics, not to mention the farm work. How was this kid thing supposed to flow with what I do for work? But I knew Dan wanted kids and figured that somewhere deep down, I did too. Perhaps it was my fear of not having a family of my own later in life, but for whatever reason, I agreed to start trying.

Failing to conceive after twelve months of trying, each of us went to our respective doctors to get checked out. We were both cleared physically; there was no health explanation at all. That didn't faze me. I figured if it were meant to be, it would happen. Either it wasn't in the cards for us or it wasn't time yet.

The emotional distance between me and Dan had been growing for some time. Then Dan started struggling with erectile dysfunction, and it was clear we were silently headed our separate ways.

When I inquired why he didn't seem to be turned on by seeing me naked, his response was, "I see you naked every day."

Damn. No response would have beat that response. *I'm quite confident there are countless men that would jump at the opportunity to take your place,* I thought, and may have even said it out loud. I don't recall.

TEMPERED GLASS

His comment should have been a *huge* red flag. Instead, I blew it off as a deflection from his own struggles. Thankfully, I never took it to heart; it never hindered my self-confidence or sense of worth, though this is a rabbit hole many women drown in. Girl, defy the lies with the truth and walk in it.

We eventually verbalized the obvious distance and decided to see a marriage counselor. We met with the counselor individually, then collectively, and he immediately hit the nail on the head when he said, "You guys make great roommates!"

Dan had a passive personality, just like my dad and John-Boy. I had just the opposite personality. I didn't really know what to make of this pattern of men in my life, other than I seemed to have a magnet drawing them to me. With them, I initiated and led almost everything or we would never see progress in anything because we'd be thinking about it for the rest of our lives. (Type A's, I hear your "Amens!")

Dan would let someone walk over him before he would create conflict. He worked a full-time job about twenty minutes away, would help me occasionally on the flip houses or at the farm after work, visit and help at

Nana and Papaw's, do his share around the house for the most part, go to races with me, and if there weren't any races that night, he would even cook.

He didn't seem to mind the time I spent at the farm, with Mav and Mary, or at the track. He was very much in his own world, going through the motions of life, never bucking anything I did or said, always compliant and supportive with or without the presence of others. He never got angry with me or the situation, that I know of. He fully trusted me and experienced firsthand the joy our newfound friends had brought. He communicated with Mav and Mary when he saw them in person but wasn't nearly as close as I was, perhaps simply due to the amount of unscheduled time and flexibility I had.

He was a good person who showed genuine care and concern for family and friends. I could tell he struggled to find his place. Growing up, he had moved around a lot and did not have the stability I was raised with. In our marriage, we had major role reversal, from sexual drive to work, skills, abilities, and income. Although I never flaunted this, I always suspected our dynamic made him feel insecure. We never fought—ever. Unfortunately, neither was there any fire or desire, nor any depth of love seven years into our marriage. We were purely coexisting—"great roommates."

Looking back, I believe I had been too young and naïve, in a hurry to live the small-town American dream and leave home. So I got married and bought a house. I never knew what love was, nor did I think I was ever actually in love with Dan. I lost my virginity to him, did life with him for eleven years, and still, I realized, I had never shed a tear over him. It took a while, but I finally came to understand I had made a mistake when I said "I do."

I remember a time just before we were married. After three long years of premarital classes and counseling, about a week before the wedding, I was sitting with my aunt in a truck in my parents' driveway. Dan was in the barnyard splitting wood to burn steam, when she asked me if I was ready for this life with him. At the last minute there had been a difficult situation for him to navigate with his family, and he was spiraling.

My aunt asked, "Are you ready to contend with these challenging dynamics with his family for the rest of your life?"

I remember thinking to myself, *No, I'm not.* I don't recall what I said out loud. I had invested three years with this man, championing his mental and emotional health. He had become a part of my family already, and I didn't have the heart or courage to break everyone else's heart. So I said, "I do."

I thought we would figure it out. We would continue to grow, and he would get stronger, putting healthy boundaries in place to protect us. We would make it work, because where I come from, you might as well consider a divorce decree your ticket to hell. I'm not an advocate for divorce by any means, no more than I'm an advocate for coexisting with someone you aren't in love with.

Here is what I wished I had known or someone had told me: Ladies, you will never change or fix a man no more than he will change or fix you. Save yourself and him by having the courage to call it off before you say "I do" if there is any doubt whatsoever that he is the one for you or that his family is for you. Break whosever heart you need to break to save them and you the future pain and hassle of divorce. Broken hearts will keep beating, and they can heal if they so choose. He, nor his family, nor your family is your burden to bear. You are responsible for you. You can only change you. Do not deliberately set yourself up to fail by convincing yourself things will change, or that he will change or grow out of anything. Perhaps it means taking more time and seeking yet more wise counsel before you commit to a lifetime together. I regret not doing so myself. I regret not acting on the reality of truth I faced internally that night in the driveway. I regret not breaking hearts only three years into a dating relationship as opposed to nearly a decade of marriage. I wasted a lot of life going through the motions, simply coexisting rather than living the abundant life God has called us to. Be brave, be courageous, and follow your instinct.

> # YOU ARE RESPONSIBLE FOR YOU. YOU CAN ONLY CHANGE YOU.

All of this was going on in the background during the time I was getting to know Mav and Mary. I found my newfound business partner and friend, Mav, to be as discontented as I was, if not more. We talked a lot, about a lot, and our marriages were no exception. It was a safe space with him—no pressure, no biases, no expectations, only support and encouragement. Sometimes it was deep and other times we kept it light.

We were headed to the vet's clinic once again, one hot summer day, and it was over an hour away. Never a dull moment, we each had a quick-witted, sarcastic air that curated lots of laughs, banter, and warm fuzzy feelings. I recall it being an exceptionally fun conversation and ride that day when he reached over from the driver's seat and patted and rubbed the inside of my thigh, which was fully exposed from simply sitting in my blue Nike running shorts. I've obviously never been severely electrocuted as I'm here to share this story, but can I tell you "electric" was exactly how I felt when he touched me. Hand on thigh. That's it. He had to swing into a gas station before we arrived, for which I was grateful, because I feared the blue Nike shorts wouldn't conceal the evidence of being electrified!

It was a confusing but not uncomfortable ride home. We pulled in, took the long, slow ride down my drive, came to a stop, and jumped out like every time before to begin unloading groggy horses. One out, two out, and I felt his hand reaching for my shoulder from behind. A slow, gentle turn, my back now to the trailer wall, my mind spinning, my heart racing, and my body electric. I vaguely recall uttering the words, "We can't do this—you're married, I'm still married…holy shit!" Our first embrace, fully clothed; I'd never been with a man equipped like that. In fact, I'd only been intimate with one man in my entire life: my ever-so-fading husband, and he was mowing the yard just a couple hundred feet away. As we finished unloading, Mav said, "Hey, if that's all that happens, it's okay, it was fun. Just take time to think about it."

I watched him pull away and proceeded to take care of the chores as Jennifer Nettles's song "Playing with Fire" came on.

I wanna flirt with my own fear,
Wanna dance with my desire

Glory, hallelujah, and amen!

CHAPTER 4

THE AWAKENING

WHAT WAS THERE to think about? I had lost the best friend I'd ever had, John-Boy, to a jealous wife two years prior, and I didn't want to lose another. I was okay with my dying marriage and stoked for every second I had to do life with Mav.

I knew right from wrong. I grew up in church, a church that completely negated me when they castrated my friend and coddled his wife. I remember thinking at the time, *God, if this is what this church thing is all about and this is how your people are, I want nothing to do with it!*

After Mav's touch in that Ford truck and our embrace in the trailer, playing with fire sounded like the perfect prescription for a gal hungry for fun and excitement. What was there to think about?

More than I knew at the time. The enemy is out to steal, kill, and destroy. It's perplexing how sometimes the devil uses God's own people and church to create space for his own evil intent. I wholeheartedly believe the church is a hospital for sinners rather than a sanctuary for saints. I also believe two things can be true at the same time. I don't doubt that the very people who failed my friends John-Boy and Jenni loved Jesus, but they didn't have the courage to do the harder right. As a result, I was morally abandoned by the very leaders, volunteers, and staff that I had worked and worshipped alongside for nearly two decades. When you haven't done anything wrong, with God as your witness, and yet you are pretty much condemned for pursuing the harder right, it creates a gap—a very wide gap.

Mav became my closest confidant and friend. He became my safe haven, and I became his.

There wasn't anything we didn't talk about, joke about, or reminisce on. We were two of a kind but not working on a full house—yet. On the rare occasion we weren't working together in person, you could bet the

THE AWAKENING

farm that we were on the phone or texting throughout the day. We enjoyed our work, especially when we could do it together. It felt surreal. Life was grand when we met, but now I felt my life was the best it had ever been! In talking with Mav, nothing was off limits, including our personal and sexual lives. We had created a safe space, and we knew it without even saying it.

I know, I see you, bright shining red flag. And I also see you, Mr. Cowboy Boots, with your ball cap and Ray-Bans, twice my age, cool and collected, rolling along, singing a song, and *looking* forty (per my aunt B).

Mav showed up not a minute too soon, not a minute too late, just in time to fill the gap in my life. And I'm here to tell you, Mav's presence, personality, and overall demeanor made the hurt and loss of my church and friends feel like a thing of the past, something that happened long, long ago. I still missed John-Boy, but I wasn't living in devastation. I was in the gain, flying high, feeling like I was living my *best* life.

The enemy is sneaky like that. He will stop at nothing, using even good things and people to accomplish his mission to steal, kill, and destroy.

Four days after that first touch, Mav and I arranged

to meet after our morning work. I went back to my barn, and he met me there.

He got out of the truck and asked, "Are you sure you want to do this?"

> **THE ENEMY IS SNEAKY LIKE THAT. HE WILL STOP AT NOTHING, USING EVEN GOOD THINGS AND PEOPLE TO ACCOMPLISH HIS MISSION TO STEAL, KILL, AND DESTROY.**

I handed him a condom and said, "I've never been more sure of anything in my life." I was smiling from ear to ear as we walked through the dirt-floor barn.

He followed me up the steps to the living quarters. I ventured into the master bedroom while he ran to the restroom. He turned the corner and seemed surprised.

"Is everything alright?" I asked.

THE AWAKENING

"Yes, I guess I've just never been with such a confident woman," he said as I climbed onto the bed fully naked and exposed in the light of day.

As crazy as it is to say out loud now, we had discussed this as a "I help you, you help me" encounter. The plan was to go up and have sex, not to engage in some intimate or romantic retreat by peeling back a layer at a time in the dark of night with nothing but the moonlight shining in.

Still, I, too, was in awe of what I was looking at, including a gray hair or two. A little "crazy" that added to the thrill and unbelievability of it all. He looked and felt like nothing I had ever experienced before.

It was so good, in fact, that Mav thought I was climaxing and let himself go. The conflicting expression of absolute pleasure on his face is one I will never forget. He felt terrible when I didn't lie and instead told him, "No, I didn't climax with you. I was just enjoying the moment."

He clapped his hands quickly, and said, "Sorry. Like a damn rabbit, I was off!"

We laughed, erased our traces, and regrettably had to go.

From that day forward, I had never known such a selfless man behind closed doors. I couldn't get enough and neither could he. This was a man who could be standing ten feet away in a shedrow (the space between horse stalls), and I'd catch one glance and feel the electric rush through my body as if we had full-body contact. Nothing turned me on faster than seeing his silhouette walking down the shedrow of a four-hundred-foot barn in his Wranglers and boots with only the light of day beaming in. It was picture perfect, magazine material minus the Stetson hat, and he was holding me every chance we got.

I've had sex with two men in my life, my husband and Mav. My wedding night was painful and far from bliss. But this morning rendezvous had sent me to the moon, chasing all the stars, and I didn't even get off. Could it be the beginning of a genuine awakening?

One evening after dinner I was struggling to get everything cleaned up and put away because of his constant harassment and interruptions, which I didn't mind the least bit. Physical touch is my number one love language, and though Mav never took the test, I'm quite certain it was his. I don't remember how much time had passed since our prior rendezvous, but it had been a minute. Frankly, I'm surprised we even ate dinner.

THE AWAKENING

I turned on some music, lit a candle, and turned all the lights off. Standing in the kitchen, I asked, "Can you dance?"

"Oh, girl, we shouldn't be a doin' this," he whispered as I reached for his waistline.

Confused, I said, "I can't dance on my feet, so you gotta lead." What was so bad about sharing a dance on our feet in light of the many dances we were sharing in bed? I wondered.

What did he know that I didn't? He had thirty years on me, and he wasn't one to quickly state his mind with full transparency. This night was no exception. We shared a little two-step in the kitchen. I'm not sure we made it through a full song before he led me straight into my bedroom.

He had some "quirks," for lack of a better term. He didn't want to make out for fear of falling in love. I laughed it off like it was the dumbest thing I'd ever heard.

He'd laugh, and remark, "Haven't you ever seen *Pretty Woman*?"

He didn't like his head touched either; neck, perfectly okay, but not the hair.

So strange, but I respected his wishes for the most part—or at least tried to. Sometimes the heat of the moment would make us both forget his wishes. As for me, it was a free-for-all; there was nothing off limits. He had all of me: mind, body, and heart. And I didn't even know it.

I vividly remember going to dinner with Mav and a group of people, and all he'd have to do is gently press his boot onto my boot under the table to light a fire—a fire that on most of those nights he couldn't put out. It would burn and build until we could find a way to sneak away. The ecstasy of our extramarital affair kept us on a constant high. Our minds were always racing and running trying to formulate the next window of opportunity while consistently pouring a little gas on it every time we talked or crossed paths.

One time I texted him, "Bring your cowboy hat." Regrettably, he didn't have it with him. I was excited to mix things up and rock his world. I went to the bathroom to slip into a see-through black lace lingerie-style dress that stopped about mid-thigh with his favorite red lace thong below. I had black cowboy boots with high heels and a zipper that ran all the way up to my knee. I was just missing his hat to complete the look. I remembered his anthem, "Take the good with the bad," and decided to roll

THE AWAKENING

with it. I walked into the bedroom, sheepishly smiling as I anticipated his reaction.

"Oh my gosh, girl," he exclaimed as he reached for me to pull me on the bed. "Leave your boots on." Thankfully, there weren't any spurs attached.

Whether it was a pinch, pat, compliment, or sexy remark, we dared not let opportunities pass us by to bring a little heat. We had a code for condoms. One of us would ask, "Did you check the waterers?" If the response was "yes," it meant we had a condom and were ready for the next opportunity that came. That stopped when we decided not to fool with condoms anymore.

We got comfortable with the fire we were playing with and where we played with it. If our homes were occupied, we'd try not to get too sweaty during our morning work and squeeze in a little action before we loaded hay in old barns, which I worried might have the best wireless cameras on the planet in the middle of no-man's-land. I wasn't as worried in the Amish barns, but we were both too chicken there for fear of kids crawling out of the woodwork. Looking back, of all the places we braved, those barns were probably some of the safest in the world!

MORE THAN A SECRET

The time between racing seasons were the hardest. I'd help haul horses south in late fall and help bring them back early spring. Mav would spend most of the winter in the south training while I stayed home and took care of the farm, watching over the older horses turned out to pasture, mares, and babies. We occasionally hauled at the same time in different trucks to maximize the move, and sometimes he sent me solo. If he didn't have company riding along, we would try to time a trip so we could land at the same hotel, still booking two rooms and sharing one. Crazy, I know, and we fought about it, but that was part of "playing it safe" for Mav.

I got a good laugh the first time I passed a Kum & Go gas station hauling horses. I called him and asked, "Are you vested in a business I don't know about, or did they just name the gas station after you?" We had to laugh to keep from crying, because it was indeed our reality more often than not.

One winter, Mav seemed down and lonely, so I drove across the state line to catch a flight and surprise him for the weekend. He figured it out before I got on the plane. He knew me a little too well. I was in a hurry when he called, trying to get gas so I could make it to the airport

THE AWAKENING

in time. I think he heard the panic in my voice, and I told him I would call him back because I was about to run out of gas, which should have taken ten minutes at best, right? But the truth was, I also needed to get in the airport and through security.

Sure enough, he was calling me again. I never missed his calls, come hell or high water, and if I did, I immediately called him back. It threw a red flag; he said he wanted to let me know Mary was off her rocker in case she came by or called me.

As I write this story for the first time since living it, I see so many subtle shifts that I didn't even know were happening at the time. I booked a flight, drove three hours to catch it, and boarded a plane that at the time sent my blood flowing backward to get to him, not for sex, not for physical satisfaction, but for comfort. I wanted to show up in hopes that it would lift him from the sadness and dismay he was experiencing.

Our relationship had quickly become more than "I help you, you help me," but I was oblivious. He was tugging my heartstrings, and I would respond with sacrificing my own comfort to bring him comfort in the loneliness of winter training from afar.

According to Mav, Mary was "falling off her rocker" more and more as suspicion grew.

I said, "Well, I don't know what to do."

He asked, "What do you mean?"

"I am about to get on a plane. I was planning to surprise you for the weekend. Should I stay here?"

"Well, no, I don't think there's any chance of her coming down here," he remarked in shock.

He met me at a hotel, pleasantly surprised and overjoyed. We went to the nearest steakhouse, and then a saloon with a dance floor nearby, both of us at the height of our glory. We had never braved going out together locally; it was too risky. Mav paid to get us in and got one drink before we had to leave. I got food poisoning and threw up the rest of the night. We made the best of it, and it was the only two nights in our entire affair that we didn't have to set an alarm for work or to dodge suspected spies or people we knew.

To date, these couple of years will go down as two of the most exciting and fun years of my life. I was having the time of my life: Business was good; we were winning at the track; and we took every opportunity we found for an early-morning rendezvous or "afternoon delight" (as he would call it). Once in a great while, we shared an evening for takeout and three-fourths of a night to roll in the hay.

For the first time in my life, I knew what all the hype and fuss was about. Mav sent me to the moon and showed me all the stars, leaving me wanting to go back before he ever pulled out of the drive. Sex was the best it had ever been.

Yes, you read that right. I was living in sin and having the time of my life. The enemy is a master manipulator!

It wasn't easy to navigate; sleeping with one eye open and parking in the back forty was never fun in a torrential downpour or foot of snow at 3 a.m. to be sure I was gone before the grooms knew the world was spinning. And if Mav came my way, he was usually restless, fearing who might show up at his place while he was MIA. But we did it anyway. Neither of us slept much, and we didn't care. We ran on adrenaline and the thrill of our ever-evolving and undeniable flame.

We were together a lot, and I didn't want it any other way. I had never felt more alive and connected to someone in my life—mentally, emotionally, and now physically. I've since learned that intimacy is built on unscheduled time; I couldn't agree more.

Neither of us had any intention of getting divorced when the affair began, which is why I didn't leave Dan for Mav. I left Dan *because of* Mav. This man had removed the mask of my naïveté of what a deep connection, both emotional and physical, really was. I was awakened to a desire to see, talk to, and spend as much time together as possible, a desire I had never experienced before or during my marriage.

Dan had been resisting the divorce, mostly out of fear of what the future would hold for him and stepping away from the family that had embraced and loved him so well. We scheduled to meet and discuss our situation in the barn on a Sunday afternoon.

To my pleasant surprise, he stopped by a day or two prior and said, "I'm good with it. Go ahead and file."

I did. We were amicable throughout, and it was final in July. Come January, my dad saw on Facebook that Dan had a baby. I was at the farm and Mav was pushing up manure when I got the news. I shared, and then I texted Dan and congratulated him. The puzzle pieces were starting to fit together. Perhaps it wasn't a health issue after all but rather another woman. It didn't matter. He got the kid he always wanted, and I was having the time of my life playing with fire.

THE AWAKENING

Mary was growing increasingly jealous of the connection we had, suspicion running high. Behind closed doors Mary was threatening Mav with World War III. He assured me we would get through this.

I felt that this man, far from passive, fought for me like no one ever had, probably because no one has ever had to!

I don't know who was flying higher, him or me. I loved helping him, loved working with the horses, loved having someone who believed I could do *anything*. Mav trusted me with his nicest horses, best equipment, trucks, and even foaling out mares as an amateur.

I had forgotten how much I loved being part of a winning team, with a leader that championed me *big*! The races were an adrenaline rush. We would dream about how big we could grow the business with both of us working it, build another barn, and maybe run at more tracks. I loved the social life, sitting trackside on a beautiful evening, having a drink, and going to eat afterward. He pulled me in every chance he had. He gave me more and more responsibility, which, little did we know at the time, inspired a natural progression of Mary feeling left out and isolated. Mav asked me to go everywhere, taught me nearly everything I know as it relates to horses, including not to wear a wedding band when you're dealing with shanks every day. I'm still not sure if that was genuine or strategic advice.

We even started dreaming about places we'd like to go, things we'd like to see and do together. We were building a life we didn't have the freedom to live—yet. The excitement and hope kept us going, grinding through each day with vigor. Despite not loving construction, Mav liked making money, and I thought it might help calm the tension if Mary and I had more to communicate and work on together. So Mary and Mav even invested in some homes to flip with me. We all made money, but it didn't help the quickly spiraling and volatile situation.

Perhaps you're judging my attempt to engage Mary while masquerading our affair. I'm not suggesting I was right. In fact, I was wrong on countless fronts in our situation. We were all still working and doing life together. I was feeling so wanted by one person, and I was secretly despised by his wife who continued to engage me like nothing was wrong. Mary continued to invite me to eat, have a drink, and more while fighting with Mav behind

THE AWAKENING

closed doors. My aim was peace, to live as amicably as possible without hurting or losing Mav. So I did the only thing we had successfully shared in the beginning. I asked them to join me on a project.

The harder Mary fought, the louder she screamed, the tighter Mav held on to me. I received a text from Mary asking if I went with him one day on a different vet trip. I said yeah, and showed the text to Mav.

He called Mary and said, "I asked if you wanted to go."

I could hear her response: "I know it's fine. I just didn't know if Alicia went."

It wasn't fine. One time, Mav found out Mary had called the secretary at the vet's office just to see if I was with him. It got to the point that she would make up stories that I felt were nothing more than lame attempts to create a divide between us, to try to make him mad at me. That never worked either.

I didn't need help making him mad. She just never knew it. He could bring out the best in me and the worst in me, especially when it came to how he handled this difficult situation. He would call early in the morning or head in the direction I would be driving to pick up my first load of horses, meet me on the road, and ask me to "lay low for a few days" or "let the storm pass."

This began taking a toll. I never knew when the storm was going to brew, but I knew it was stirring more frequently.

CHAPTER 5

SECRET REALITY

AMID ALL THE escalating tension, my body began to react in ways I had never experienced. My left leg had been numb from the knee down for two months when I finally decided I should go get it checked out. I went to a chiropractor first and got an MRI. They called asking me to come in. The doctor seemed unusually concerned.

"You have a thirteen millimeter L5 S1 herniation lying on your sciatica. If you don't do something very soon, you are going to have permanent nerve damage in your left leg and foot."

"What are my options?" I asked.

"I can refer you to a surgeon. Statistically you will have a 50 percent chance at a successful surgery your first time, or we can set you up to do decompression therapy for an hour a day, five days a week, for eight weeks. If the herniation successfully shrinks, you will avoid surgery altogether. By the way, you will not be able to lift more than a gallon of milk for the next two months at best."

I was flipping out internally.

Didn't he hear what I did for work? On average I picked up at least five to ten fifty-pound bags of feed a day, and that didn't even take into account the hay, water, horse legs, lumber, or any other material on my flips that I lift and move daily.

I'm thirty years old and back surgery? A 50 percent chance of success sounds terrible! Eight weeks, thirty minutes each way, an hour on the table, two hours a day?

I hated this. The additional workload that would be put on Mav made my whole body cringe. There were certain things he didn't let anyone else do; it was me or him. What was worse was that this was completely out of my control, which sucked for an admitted control freak!

Now, not only was I mentally and emotionally stressed, but I was about to be physically tanked. I had lived with a numb leg for two months, but it was to the point that the sciatic nerve was firing regularly, and the pain was unbearable. I've always been a fighter and been told I have a high pain tolerance, but I felt like a wuss when that pain hit. Tears would just roll, and I couldn't stop them.

I was on a lifting restriction, but surely, I thought, I could still contribute by hauling for Mav as long as I had someone ready to load and unload for me. Well, not so simple. The herniation was on my left side. Sometimes I could put my left foot up on the dash and other times that would trigger the pain. I would have to cross my left leg over my right leg to get pressure off my left hip and glute. Sounds like a safe way to drive, right, especially pulling a trailer full of horses?

Mav and I were two years into our friendship, working relationship, and affair. My physical state burdened me more out of concern and care for Mav than it ever did myself. It killed me that I couldn't flip a switch to fix this, that I couldn't fix my body or suck up the pain indefinitely. This wasn't going away without a drastic change in my daily work activities. I legit felt like the "delicate flower" we had sarcastically called each other whenever either of us showed any sign of weakness.

Mav was understanding. He never gave me shit over

my back, and he was super cautious in bed not to fire the nerve. He was gentle and cared for me to the extent that he could, given our situation.

This lifestyle was exhausting. I was discovering that being someone's number two takes a massive mental and physical toll, and I found it difficult to articulate in words. Living as a secret mistress was sucking the life out of me.

I vividly remember standing (less painful than sitting) in the treatment room with four white walls, tight-knit carpet, gown on in preparation for some X-rays, glaring at the posters on the wall while waiting for the chiropractor to come in. One poster stood out. I don't remember the details, but it illustrated how much mental and emotional stress impacts one's physical body and health. I remember thinking to myself, *No wonder I have a thirteen-millimeter disc herniation*. But I never admitted any stress to the doctors or anyone else except Mav.

Mav knew the toll our situation was taking on both of us, but short of walking away from each other or him abruptly filing for divorce, we didn't have a solution. So we navigated the turmoil, stress, and unrelenting desire to be together the best we knew how.

SECRET REALITY

I still loved the work, I loved our friendship, connection, and benefits, I loved the thrill of the sport. I hated being number two.

I can still hear the echo of his voice to this day: "We have to take the good with the bad—it is what it is."

Mary was becoming increasingly suspicious, although she never voiced that to me. I heard all about it through Mav. Because of her suspicions, she left town less and less. And even when she did, Mav was convinced she had people watching his every move, maybe even a hired PI.

Waiting until dark in the dead of summer to meet meant we skipped dinner altogether and only had a few short hours before the day started again. By this point, our go-to restaurant, in a semi-bad part of an adjoining town, which we figured was a pretty safe bet where nobody that knew us would go, had closed its doors. Mav was too scared of being seen almost everywhere else, and so most often, one or both of us went to pick up Mexican, burgers from the pub, country fried chicken dinners from the local steakhouse, or I cooked his favorite, spaghetti, if it was early enough in the evening, and we ate in the comfort of my home or his living quarters.

MORE THAN A SECRET

Looking back, the lengths we went to do life together is perplexing. If I lay in his bed the night prior, one of us was running into the living quarters between chores the next morning to get his briefs and sheets washed and bed made back up just in case Mary showed up. Not as big of a deal for someone working in an office, I suppose, but it was a pain walking in from a dirt-floor barn or shit-covered horse trailer to erase our traces and make everything spotless despite being filthy from the morning work. However, I believe the extreme effort we both went to contributed to the joy and ecstasy we felt when in each other's company. A dose of each other, whether by text, phone, or sex, left us longing for more.

When we did roll the dice and go out to dinner, I knew Mav couldn't fully enjoy it for being paranoid of being seen. Mary had put a stop to our riding in the same truck by now, because "it didn't look good." She had also imposed a dress code on me (pawning it off on Mav, but I obviously knew better) that I couldn't wear shorts to the track anymore because "it didn't look good," though Mary wore shorts on occasion. Mary had also put a hard stop on us not going out to eat by ourselves.

SECRET REALITY

I'll never forget the straw that broke the camel's back on the latter. She was in their home state, and he and I were heading that way to help get their homeplace in order. I was going to tile a shower for them. Mav and I had worked for hours to get the farm organized in order for us to leave. We were even surprising Mary with hauling the equipment back to get the pastures mowed and manicured. Mav and I hadn't eaten all day and it would be late by the time we arrived, and so we stopped for dinner on our way. I could hear the fight over it from the bedroom above theirs late into the night. Though Mary never verbalized it to me, I got the sense I was still welcome to slave away and help Mav at the farm, house, or anywhere in between and run horses, but I couldn't share a meal with him.

Mary loved and cared for Mav. She saw his workload, and she knew how much I was relieving the burden on him day in and day out, probably more so than anyone else that had ever worked with or for them up to that point. Plus, I wasn't on payroll.

As much as she suspected a growing connection between me and Mav—and despised it—I got the impression that Mary didn't want to interfere with the good thing we had on the business side of the equation. Her solution was to try to put these boundaries in place, even though they were nearly impossible to accommodate as closely as Mav and I worked together. I had pretty much become his right hand.

We were stuck. Mary didn't want to lose my help but didn't want me around Mav so much. Mav didn't want to lose me, but he didn't want to lose everything he had worked for his whole life either by filing for divorce without her being in agreement to do so.

By this point, I felt like Mary wanted to use me for what I could do for them. Mav saw it, despised it, but didn't do anything about it so as not to raise suspicion or start World War III.

Although we never got caught having dinner together after that, sometimes she would FaceTime him using the grandkids as an excuse, and he would rush to his farm as soon as we could get on the road so he could return the FaceTime call and not raise questions. He would claim he fell asleep or had his phone charging, only to hang up and reconvene with me.

I was becoming sick and tired of playing the games, fueling the lies, and getting ditched on a moment's notice.

SECRET REALITY

Other times, a horse owner would stop by the farm unannounced, and because Mav never went anywhere or did anything in the evenings after races when he was alone (so everyone thought), this made it hard for Mav to get away without raising questions, since many of these owners communicated with Mary too.

There were times Mav would be at my place and get a call from Mary. She wanted to talk, and it would turn into a fight. I vividly remember him walking back in my bedroom after one fight, remarking, "I could walk away from her and never look back."

Even if they weren't fighting, whether I was at his place or he at mine or we were staying in a hotel, Mav would make a routine call to Mary about the same time each night when she would be expecting him to turn in for the night.

He would say, "Let me get this over with so we can relax," and then step out. Even though I wanted the cat out of the bag, all the cards on the table, I didn't feel like it was my place to do that. So I followed his lead, and we continued the vicious cycle.

For a while, when he was super paranoid about someone catching him from his sphere of influence, so

MORE THAN A SECRET

I would meet him at a flip house to park his truck in the garage. We would then go to my place for a few hours and then back out in the wee hours of the night for him to get his truck. One night, I was pulling in the driveway of one of my flips to open the garage door so Mav could pull in and then ride with me back to my place. My phone rang, and I looked, wondering who would be calling so late. It was my mom.

"Hello?" I answered with anxious curiosity.

"Hey, the neighbor called our office and said a vehicle pulled in the drive at your flip and was sitting in front of the garage in a small truck," Mom said.

"Okay, I'll go check it out."

I hung up and got out of the truck to talk to the neighbor who was outside and assured him everything was okay. Mav was agitated, saying something along the lines of, "I'm going home; we can't keep doing this; we're going to get caught."

I pleaded otherwise, but nonetheless, it made for a great flat tire that night! Other times, we would have plans to grab dinner and spend a relaxing evening together after the races, but then I'd get a text or call: "Guess who just showed up at the track?" Ditched again.

SECRET REALITY

Mav was stressed trying to juggle it all. Although he despised my saying this to him, I felt like nothing short of a secondhand bitch—not in terms of sex, but just life in general. Sure, early on in our affair I would wonder, because he would pull back after one or two in case she "checked" him, emphasizing, "We have to take the good with the bad." If I go the rest of my life and never hear that line again, I will be elated.

We talked about the situation until we were blue in the face. He would comment, "I'm sixty years old and never in my life have I had a problem I couldn't resolve."

"What are we going to do?" I'd ask.

"I don't want to do this without you," he would say. "I don't want to lose you, and she's not open to separating." He was dead set on achieving an amicable separation and divorce from Mary, out of fear that in a conflict he would lose what he had worked for his whole life, including his kids and grandkids.

Mary could be vindictive, and she illustrated that one day behind closed doors when she took a bag of cash and dumped it, remarking something along the lines of, "This is what you will have left!"

Mav was old school and believed the man should be

the family's provider. Despite my offer, he wasn't willing to rely on me financially, not even for a season. I would say, "No judge is going to give her everything and leave you hanging dry."

He would respond, "That's if it ever made it to the judge. I've had buddies get tangled up with attorneys for so long that there was nothing left by the time they went to court."

I saw Mav as a fearless man—until it came to the subject of possibly starting over in life and business. It was too much for him. I knew it, and I saw it. I also knew that although he didn't spend a lot of time with his kids, he was fearful they might turn on him and he would therefore lose his grandkids if he initiated a divorce.

At first, he would say that after his marriage was over, if I wasn't welcome, he wouldn't go to family functions. But the more he contemplated life without his kids and grandkids, the colder his feet got to end his marriage. Naturally, I understood. I wouldn't want to lose my sister or my niece because of a significant other. Common sense would seem to indicate that the next step, then, was for us to let go of each other. It simply wouldn't work. But my "heart sense" said, *That's the*

SECRET REALITY

dumbest idea you've ever had. Don't let go of someone you care so deeply about.

Mav was meeting me on the road in the early-morning hours every two to three weeks, asking me to steer clear and lay low for a few days to let Mary cool off.

This time was no exception, but I wasn't willing to take it any longer. I said, "Yes, I'll steer clear but I'm not coming back unless this is resolved once and for all."

That was my last day helping him professionally. Our affair had always been a secret. However, I as an individual, as a human being who worked with Mav and Mary, as their neighbor, was never a "secret." Until now.

My world turned upside down overnight. Horse racing, the hobby I had grown to love, was suddenly gone. The social outlet I had come to enjoy—preparing for, watching, and celebrating wins—ended overnight. Mav's daily company and banter in person were over. The time I had spent working with him was suddenly free. I was lost.

Imagine trying to sustain a friendship with someone you don't have the freedom to be friends with. You can't just pick up the phone and call at any time. You can't openly send text messages, and certainly can't just pop in to say hi or grab lunch. Literally, I would test the waters of his location or company by texting a "?" If he didn't respond or offered very few words, I knew he had company and we couldn't talk. He was my closest friend and confidant, and I had very little access to him. I was a secret.

In Mary's eyes, there was no reason for me and Mav to communicate. I wasn't helping them anymore. We didn't have any work together, and, therefore, nothing to talk about. It was disheartening to say the least, because Mary knew that Mav and I had formed a significant friendship beyond just work, affirming it in a text message one day after she and I had a heart-to-heart on their front porch.

"Ya know it just hit me. Maybe I have been a little jealous of the friendship you and Mav share. But it's certainly not meant to hurt anyone. Not too many people get lucky enough to have someone like you. I'm sorry for hurting everyone. Never meant to. This just hit me like a ton of bricks. Lol."

I only wish that had been the end of her jealousy, but it consumed her and she never did get a grip on it. Perhaps she didn't care anymore.

I jumped on a dating app looking for nothing more than some people to meet and hang out with to get outside of my four walls. Mav was visiting one afternoon a

SECRET REALITY

couple of months later, and we were on my porch when I told him I had met a couple of guys for dinner. Mind you, I considered myself a guy's gal. I was looking for friends. I literally shook my dates' hands when we left dinner. I had always told Mav everything. Why would I hide this? I didn't think anything of it.

But did he ever! I had never seen him so upset with me, pacing my porch, lashing out, finally calming down enough to say, "Alicia, I can't believe you don't see this. I have fallen in love with you."

I was speechless. I didn't know what to say. I had no idea. I had been with Dan a total of eleven years when I divorced, and clearly didn't know what love was. Perhaps deep down I knew I loved Mav too, but I had never given the idea any space, let alone verbalized it. After all, this began as "I help you, you help me," with no intention of either of us getting a divorce, let alone entertaining a love relationship.

Mav asked me to give him the winter to get things resolved. He didn't want all the drama at the track during the meet.

Of course, I agreed to hold out for him, not to go on anymore "dinner dates," as he called them.

Winter came and went. He still thought the solution was to have an amicable separation and then divorce, but Mary made it clear that it was not possible. It was far from an *amicable* idea. I was devastated. I was trying to let go of him so I could move on with my life, but it was like he had set a hook so deep in my heart and soul that my best and strongest effort wasn't enough to get it out. Perhaps this is love's grip. Maybe I had fallen in love for the first time in my life—with a married man! Holy shit.

You don't know what you don't know. Love is a mysterious thing, and until I experienced trying to walk away from Mav, a man I knew I cared a great deal about, I didn't even recognize it for what it was. I had always told my ex-husband I loved him. I thought I did. But isn't it interesting that I never once felt any emotion or shed a tear over our separation and divorce? Mav, on the other hand, had me discovering feelings and emotions that I didn't know I was even capable of experiencing.

I mentioned earlier, Mav could bring out the best in me and the worst in me. When we weren't fighting about how to handle the situation, we were making mad love, laughing, working, giving each other shit,

SECRET REALITY

and having the time of our lives. When circumstances didn't allow us to see each other, it was hell on earth. Mav handled it one way, but I thought he should handle it another way. I was ditched, belittled, and degraded more times than I care to recall, all in the name of him saving face and pacifying people. It was exhausting, no life for either of us to continue living—but neither of us wanted to let go.

I had never understood women who stayed in abusive relationships. I always thought, there's how many million men on this planet and you're going to stay with one who beats you up? To be crystal clear, Mav *never* physically abused me. But for the first time I understood how a known hell could be more appealing than a possible unknown heaven. It reminds me of Romans 7:15–25 where Paul said he wanted to do what was good and right, but he didn't. He seemed to do what he hated.

Our life was familiar. It had good parts. I tried to take the good with the bad. Only now I understood how deeply the hook can be sunk in the human heart, how deep-seated all the tentacles were. The thought of letting go was as brutal, if not more than, the pain of remaining in the relationship. I was spiraling often. I struggled to function long enough to even stop by a jobsite. I'd get back in the truck and start bawling my eyes out once again. Hiding the pain and stress from everyone in the world was exhausting.

> **BUT FOR THE FIRST TIME I UNDERSTOOD HOW A KNOWN HELL COULD BE MORE APPEALING THAN A POSSIBLE UNKNOWN HEAVEN.**

I just wanted it all to be okay. I just wanted him to resolve his situation so we could live the rest of our lives together. But it wasn't happening, despite him telling me that he didn't want to continue running horses without me. It wasn't the same. He wasn't enjoying it. He was exhausted trying to do it all. He *looked* exhausted. He was aging quickly, and he noticed it, but he couldn't bring himself to change. He just kept saying someone is going to get hurt, someone always does in a triangle.

SECRET REALITY

I don't think Mary helped herself in the situation either. I remember a collection box for what Mav perceived, and I assumed, to be hormone tests lying on the bathroom floor for months. Mary wasn't the most proactive problem solver; rather, she was reactive, avoiding problems until she could no longer do so. She never expressed her concerns to me directly, even upon my inquiry—instead misleading me by pretending everything was fine. She only expressed her worries and displeasure with Mav. I am a firm believer that the abandoned spouse often plays an indirect yet pivotal role in an extramarital affair.

I wondered if there had been others before me, but Mav swore he had never stepped out on his marriage before. He confessed that he had had sex with another woman the night before his wedding but never afterward before me. I was shocked and couldn't imagine, but we were nearly four decades past that, so I dismissed it as something he did as an immature stud, panicking about being with one woman for the rest of his life. He said he knew better in our situation; he knew what consistent and ongoing sex would do. "Fool around and fall in love" had never rung so true, along with about a million other country songs I grew up singing but had never truly felt until now.

I was especially moved by Reba's infamous "Does He Love You?" My sister and I grew up giving that duet our best shot for anyone who would listen, including whoever she was dating. Mind you, I could not carry a tune in a bucket, but we had a blast and procured *lots* of laughs! I never, ever dreamed that I would actually live out these lyrics in real life.

I felt like a ball of confusion. Mav was taking steps to simplify a potential divorce and communicated with me about everything. He and Mary sold a business in their home state and then sold their homestead there. Mav purchased another home in the same community Mary's parents lived in, but he put it in her name only, or so I was told. Supposedly the same thing happened with her car. When the lease was up, the next vehicle went in Mary's name exclusively. When Mary wouldn't quit interrogating him and making remarks about his phone records, he pulled his number off the family plan and got his own plan.

I could go on and on about the things he was doing that gave me confidence he was eventually going

SECRET REALITY

to resolve the situation. The only red flag for me was that horses were still going under her name. It was a business move, but it would certainly complicate matters in a divorce.

It was around this time that I learned I was going to be an aunt for the first time. It hit me like a ton of bricks. My sister and I have always been super close, and I *love* kids. I was so happy for her and her husband, and our family at large. I remember going on a walk with her after learning the news. I told her I wanted to be the healthiest and coolest aunt on the planet, though "I've got some things to work through and work on." Although I'm confident she suspected it, she did not know about the affair at the time.

The magnitude of the overwhelming feelings I felt is beyond words. I didn't want to be a distraught aunt tied up in a toxic love affair. I wanted to be a healthy, fun, vibrant aunt full of life, love, and joy overflowing.

I began to wrestle with how to end the affair. I searched high and low for someone to relate to, someone who had been the mistress: How did she get out? How did she break it off? How did she muster up the courage to walk away from the deepest connection she had ever felt in her life? How do you become more than a secret? How do you tell someone goodbye that you don't want to lose? *Why* would you make such a soul-crushing move?

I came up empty-handed—nobody was talking about it from the mistress's point of view.

I loved this man. I never wanted to hurt him, never wanted to leave him, and yet he wasn't leaving her for me, despite voicing that he was still holding on to hope that he could get it resolved. I would die for this man. I would take a bullet or jump in front of a truck, whatever it took if need be. And yet, I was facing ending an affair that I knew would crush him.

I can still hear it to this day, his voice: "You're going to take away the only special thing we have left under these circumstances?"

"I don't want to, Mav. I swear I don't. This is killing me, but I can't be a secret for the rest of my life. You can leave your wife, and we can be together forever. But you won't leave, and so where does that leave me?" As a secret, I had to make the hardest and most painful decision of my life. I was scared to death at even the thought of ending the affair.

I wanted to die, but I wasn't selfish enough to

SECRET REALITY

take my own life. I wanted God to end my life. Then, I thought, I wouldn't have to hurt him by ending the affair. I wouldn't hurt from losing him or from being a belittled, degraded, ditched secret any longer. My niece would hear stories about me that would hopefully encourage her, but she wouldn't see this broken-hearted, soul-crushed, lifeless human that wrecked her own life and has no hope for the future. I didn't want to be a secret anymore, but I also didn't want to say goodbye.

Although Mav and I had talked many times about how selfish suicide was and promised each other we would never do it no matter how hard it got, I feared for Mav's life. It was a fear that lingered in my soul. I often thought, *I don't want to push him over the edge. I don't want to break his heart. I don't want to lose my person. I don't want his family to lose their beloved dad and grandpa over heartbreak from losing me. His physical life is more important than my emotional well-being. I don't want anyone to die because of me or a decision I make for me.*

Mav feared for Mary's wellbeing. He didn't want to burden his family any more than I wanted to burden his family over him. He was miserable in his marriage. He communicated often that he wanted to be with me, but he couldn't bring himself to do it. One of his family members had killed himself over a woman and that story haunted me like the plague.

CHAPTER 6

DON'T HAVE SECRETS

I DECIDED TO attend Christy Wright's Business Boutique Conference in Nashville, Tennessee, during the pandemic when everything else was at a standstill. This was just a few months after the country music legend Kenny Rogers passed away. I had been hanging out with my two-month-old niece on my sister's bed, my sister nearby folding laundry and listening in, when the news crossed the screen.

As a picture of Kenny and his family appeared, my angelic sister exclaimed, "Oh my word, how could anyone be in a relationship with that much age difference?"

I watched the screen and baby intently to avoid engaging in her shock and dismay. Dying inside, not knowing whether I wanted to laugh or cry, trying not to react at all, I thought, *They only had a twenty-eight-year gap. I will never be able to tell her about my thirty-year gap!*

The pressure was building within, and nobody knew it but me.

That fall, I arrived at the conference and found a seat right of center stage. A gal by the name of Annie F. Downs was up on stage and began discussing social media. I mostly zoned out, considering I wasn't active on social media at the time. Still, I heard her say, "Don't have secrets."

I glanced up and back down and the room went uncomfortably silent as she paused for what seemed like forever. Then she continued, "No, someone in this room needs to hear this; don't have secrets in real life, not just on social media."

You could have heard a pin drop. I scanned the room, feeling like all 2,400 eyes were on me. I went back to the Opryland hotel that night, found a bar, and drank myself drunk. It was too much. A complete stranger at a business conference with 1,200 women just called me out, telling me not to have secrets in my life.

DON'T HAVE SECRETS

"It's not healthy," Downs had said. I knew that. I knew I was in a toxic nightmare.

I knew the pain of being a secret and holding a secret far too well.

By now, not only was I a secret mistress, but I was also a secret friend. Despite Mav telling me he would stand up for our friendship, more often than not, he didn't. He just worked that much harder to maintain communication with me *in secret*.

My niece was approaching nine months old, and I had not resolved this toxic love affair. I had been trying on my own strength to figure out what to do or how to do it for months prior to attending this conference, to no avail. I searched high and low for a book written from the mistress's point of view. How does one navigate such a difficult and painful situation without telling a soul? I yearned to draw strength and inspiration from someone, anyone who had resolved their situation and come out alive. I couldn't find anything—not a book, not an article, not a podcast. *This is crazy*, I thought. *This country is full of extramarital affairs. There are books written by the abandoned spouse, but how is it possible that nobody has told their story from the lover's point of view? Am I doomed?*

With more thought, it made sense. Who wants to stand up and say, "Hey, look at me, I did a horrible thing. I slept with another woman's husband!" But the fact that nobody had didn't help me in my seemingly hopeless search for confidential answers.

There was no desirable solution. I didn't want to be a secret for the rest of my life, setting a toxic example for my niece, nor did I want to say goodbye to the very man who was now woven into the fibers of my being.

Most people carry one or two titles. Perhaps mom or dad, sister, friend, acquaintance, work affiliate, teammate, and so on. Mav, though, carried countless titles that became like tentacles intertwined with deep-seated hooks in my heart and soul. He was a friend, neighbor, lover, business partner, guide, confidant, soulmate, and without a doubt, "My Strongest Weakness." Thanks, Wynonna.

I believed death would be easier than goodbye. I believed my life was not mine to take, but I prayed, *God, in your grace, you could take my life for me!* Suicide seemed selfish, but I thought, *If I die of natural cause or an accident, well, my family could be mad at God. And God is God, so he could take it.* My body ached, my blood ran, my

DON'T HAVE SECRETS

mind raced, and my broken heart kept beating. Thanks, Lainey.

Mav called, upset that I had taken off out of town. Mary had just left for home, and I wasn't in town to make the most of that window of time. Still, part of me knew that if I hadn't left, she probably wouldn't have either—that's just the way it seemed to go. This time struck me as different. Instead of hanging around in seat number two waiting for my turn to spend time with Mav, I chose *me*. I chose to break out of my four walls and leave town—and so did Mary. In one sense, I hated that I wasn't there; in another, this was the beginning of a cold, harsh reality for both me and Mav. Because of this very conference, I decided this affair was over. I can still feel the breath leaving my chest as I type these words, four years later.

I didn't want it to be over. It *had* to be over. *I heard you, God, through Annie F. Downs, loud and clear.* I couldn't have secrets, or be a secret, and still thrive. Life was never supposed to be this way. Mav could love me and carry on with his life, but for me to love him, my life had stopped. This secret had a death grip on me.

That's the evil of a secret. You can't talk, you can't share, you can't seek counsel without breaking someone's confidence. This was a secret I was supposed to take to my grave, according to Mav.

I came up with a plan. I went back home, found a counselor, and told my sister and brother-in-law about my affair with Mav, with many tears and fears of the unknown followed by a good laugh over the Kenny Rogers parallel. My sister was mortified, saying something along the lines of, "Oh my word, I can't believe I even said that. I'm, like, the least judgmental person in the world!"

> # I COULDN'T HAVE SECRETS, OR BE A SECRET, AND STILL THRIVE.

It was no longer *my* secret.

I told Mav what happened at the conference and that I could not and would not continue the affair. I think he heard me, but I don't think he fully believed me on the phone that day. Why would he?

I had tried in my own strength multiple times that year to end the affair, only to feel the tug-of-war between my mind of logic and my heart of feelings. I had conceded to the *feelings* more times than I can recall, because who doesn't want to feel good and who doesn't want to warm the heart of someone they love? The trouble was, as good as it was, and as reassuring as it felt, reality only blasted me harder when I was right back to sleeping single in a double bed, knowing he was sharing a bed with another, even if his back was turned to her.

I'm a strong person, but I was *weak* in willpower.

Willpower is not enough in the throes of trauma.

I've heard Annie F. Downs say on multiple occasions, "Feelings can ride but they cannot drive." There came a point where I had to choose: Did I want to be a secret or did I want to say goodbye? Those were my only two options. Neither option felt right; neither option felt good; neither option was desirable to me.

It was a constant battle between my heart and my mind. Logic said, "This is toxic. *Get out!*" My heart said, "If he dies to you, you will die a long, slow, and painful death. This will *crush you!*" Did I want to be a secret or heal?

My life felt like hell on earth. I kept obsessing over what Mav had said: "You're the one that took away the only special thing we had left." I was spiraling. The same thoughts kept repeating: I had become his person and he, my person. I didn't want to let my person down, and yet I didn't want to feel like a degraded secondhand bitch anymore. I didn't want to be a secret number two. I didn't want to live a lie; it violated my own core value of integrity!

I always told Mav, "If anyone, including your wife, flat-out asks me if we are having an affair, I will not lie to them or her." Nobody ever asked. Somehow, in some jacked-up way, I had justified living the lie as long as I didn't have to *tell* the lie.

Mav always said, "This is something we will go to our graves with."

And I thought, *As long as nobody asks me.*

I felt crushed. Mav wasn't wrong. Intimacy was our escape from the stress and pressure of the situation. Without that lane of relief, peace, and satisfaction, what would we have left without the freedom of friendship? I was scared out of my mind.

I still had no idea how to move forward. How do you choose not to love someone that you love? Could I let go of a man I never wanted to let go, a man I passed on the road every single day, usually multiple times? If

DON'T HAVE SECRETS

I did let go, would I ever experience the depth of what we had again in another relationship? Would anyone else ever touch that place in my soul? Would I ever have the same natural banter, desire, and hunger I had for him with anyone else? Would I always long for him? Who would I be without my safety net? Would I feel free, or like a pretty bird still locked in a cage because my heart is not free? I'd be on my own without my person—how would I navigate lonely alone in my own home? Was this truly a "once upon a lifetime"[1] love as Mav conveyed with Alabama's song? *Please God, tell me he's wrong.*

CHAPTER 7

AMPUTATION

"It's hard to walk toward a future you don't want."

—Lysa TerKeurst
Forgiving What You Can't Forget

It was a cold December night when I walked into the counselor's office for the first time. The lobby was a bit cold, walls bland, carpentry poor. Jane, the counselor, came out and invited me into the therapy room. This room was much warmer, smaller, and inviting. We covered the basics. I told her I was a very direct person, would tell it like it is, and that I was coming to her for help, because I couldn't seem to figure out how to help myself.

After I shared my background and story, Jane explained that Mav emotionally charges me. And so, to start the healing process, or grief journey, I would need to terminate contact with Mav.

"How long?" I demanded as I felt the weight of the world settle on my shoulders. It had been less than two months since I had ended the affair, and I never, ever had any desire or intention of ending our friendship.

"Awhile," she responded.

After my first appointment, I walked out feeling defeated and painfully overwhelmed. I didn't want to lose my person altogether. Once again, the thought of a permanent goodbye made death seem more appealing.

How could I sever all connection with someone I cared so much about when I saw him every single day? Why would I? I had told him I would not be a secret any longer; however, I couldn't control what he did or how he handled it.

I went back and saw Jane the next week, feeling conflicted. This professional I had sought out for help was seemingly making things worse. She wanted me to completely disconnect, cold turkey, from my person, my soulmate, my former lover, my closest friend and

AMPUTATION

confidant. Still, she had a calm about her that drew me in amid the chaos of my life.

Jane told me I was too wonderful to be his secret. I deserved better. Mav wanted everything, but that was not fair to me. She eventually told me, "They never leave."

"What do you mean?" I inquired.

"Statistically, men who are in long-term marriages and have an affair with a younger woman never leave their marriage, despite indicating otherwise."

I didn't believe her. I didn't want to believe her. At this point, I had ended the affair because he was still married and I was a secret mistress, but with every fiber of my being I believed that he might still resolve his situation and we might still live happily ever after in the light of day—eventually. I told Mav what Jane said, and he responded in such a way that led me to believe she was full of shit, and he would prove it in time.

Note to self: When you seek wise counsel, don't dismiss the wisdom of their experience. If you do, be prepared to eat humble pie. Jane wasn't telling me what I wanted to hear, so I rejected her opinion that Mav wouldn't leave. Why would he stay? It was not a joyful, life-giving marriage—just the opposite actually. Who wants to settle for coexisting and going through the motions? Been there, done that, got the T-shirt. I wanted him to want more for himself. Frankly, I wanted Mary to want more for *herself*. I couldn't imagine wanting to remain in a marriage with a man I believed was in love with someone else.

In the meantime, my counselor told me about a church that I might be interested in. I had previously shared the foundation of faith I was raised on, the church incident in which I was morally abandoned, and my love for Jesus that really never wavered. But let's face it, it's hard to chase Jesus when you are living in sin. So, I numbed out for a few years until I couldn't deny the God check at the Business Boutique Conference.

I left my counseling session and went home to google the church. I came across a secular article about how the church went through extreme growing pains, almost closing its doors, after the current pastor took over years prior. He stood for changes that they believed would help more people find Jesus. Those changes weren't popular among all the attendees, and they lost a large percentage of the congregation. This article showed me that he had a backbone, grit, and courage. It gave me confidence, coming from an outside author, that if a situation arose

AMPUTATION

in which the church would either take an easier out or do the harder right, we would be running toward the harder right together.

Going through the situation with the church I attended for most of my life made me question every church I ever walked into again. I had known the leadership at that church for years and they still failed to do what was right. How could I trust leadership I didn't even know at a new church? That article gave me confidence even though I remained somewhat skeptical, so I gave them a chance and began attending weekend services. I had said multiple times, *I'll never be "married" to another church again.* Let me clarify—the church is the body of Christ, and I am in that body. So perhaps it is better said, I will never be a "member" of a particular building or church unit again. I will forever be in the body of Christ. Sometimes I wonder if church leadership realizes the cost of someone, even just one person, being wounded by the church. Certainly, it is not a matter to take lightly.

We got through the holidays, and then I told Mav I had to terminate communication for a while to try to get a grip on our current reality and start healing. He didn't like it, but he respected my request. From day one, it felt like

I had invited the enemy and all his cohorts to do life with me. The guilt, the longings, the wonder, the pain—it was all-consuming. I feel depressed just reading my journal entries from that time. It was the closest I could possibly relate to an addict's story. I wouldn't wish the withdrawal symptoms on my worst enemy. It felt like it was killing me, figuratively and literally.

Could one human be addicted to another human? Codependent, for sure. I drove by his home and work more times than I could count, wondering if Mav was in town. Why, I don't know. By my request, we weren't communicating, and it would only make it harder if I learned he was in town.

It was expensive, inconvenient, and often dreaded, but I kept going to counseling every single week. One night on a whiteboard in her office, Jane helped me discover and identify all the reasons this affair wasn't for me. Then we dialed in on my *biggest* why: my niece. A child that couldn't even talk yet had my heart, hook, line, and sinker. I wanted to be the best, most honest, fun, loving, grace-filled, God-fearing aunt on the planet for her. Without uttering a word, my niece inspired me to keep fighting for my life, to hang on with a death grip

AMPUTATION

through the wind and waves, and to keep my feet planted in the fire through the forging. I had never felt so much pain in my life, especially without Mav's shoulder to cry on and soul to confide in.

It's fair to say that when we go through hard times, especially loss, we gravitate to those we are closest to. Perhaps one reason death seemed like it would be easier was because terminating contact with Mav would remove my closest confidant. Choosing to walk away and not have him to lean on or draw comfort from was incomprehensible.

Mav lived only a few miles away from my property, and pretty much no matter where I was headed, odds were high I would see him. I was coming back from the home improvement store when I saw the tractor moving in the front hay barn closest to the road. Instinctively, I swung into the driveway. He had a cab on the tractor. I walked up, and he looked over, surprised.

He opened the cab door, and I asked, fighting emotion, "How are you doing?"

"Not good," he said. He climbed down. I really don't remember what all was said. He glanced toward the apartment, stepped back, and we embraced.

I walked to my truck, tears flowing, heart aching, and left. We had survived seventy-five days of silence. I decided I never wanted to go through that again.

Mav and I struggled to learn how to live in this new light and old place. I desperately wanted to maintain a friendship and neighborly relationship. He desperately wanted to hold on to anything we could. It was increasingly difficult for him to communicate with me and especially visit me, because Mary had grown to despise me. I hadn't been a part of their farm operations for two years by then. So what need was there for us to talk?

There was this thread of hope still hanging on long after the affair ended. For years Mav had ridiculed the idea of us still being "friends," asking me, "Who are you kidding?" But now, he was trying to embrace the idea of us being friends, at least until his belief turned into reality.

He was notorious for sending me text messages along the lines of, "You're the first thing I think of every morning and the last thing before I go to sleep at night. I just can't help but believe something won't happen."

AMPUTATION

I sent him the song "Friends" by Tyler Braden:

When you say you wanna be friends . . .
Like "I love you" is something we ain't ever said.

To which he reciprocated with "Try Losing One," also by Tyler Braden:

Try living with knowing that you let her down. . . .
Try losing one.

I sent another song with the same title, "Friends," by Spencer Crandall:

We should've stayed friends.
Yeah, we should've never gave in.

Who were we kidding?
We were a mess.
It was almost like, if he was logical, I was on an emotional roller coaster, and in my logical moments he was spiraling. The most difficult days found both of us in a state of mass confusion, heartache, and pain. Other days I wonder if we were both just numb, going through the motions, trying to keep our focus on the task in front of

us. We would wave in passing, text an FM radio station on a whim to catch a song, and send songs via text. Music has always been therapeutic for me, and this season was no different. We were navigating life as we now knew it, the best we could without romantically loving each other or killing each other.

It had been about a year and a half since the affair ended. I was no longer in counseling. I felt like we had reached a place where every session seemed like a repeat of the last. So I decided to try life on my own again. That was when I received a personal invitation to attend a small business conference in North Carolina.

My purpose in going was to show up and offer support for a speaker who would be returning to the marketplace and speaking for the first time since it had been publicized that he had an extramarital affair. This was someone who had made an impact on me and my business over a decade earlier. And now he had taken the same fall I did, though my affair was not yet public. Since I had the opportunity and time to show up, armed with empathy and support, I would.

However, upon arriving, I learned that this individual wouldn't be there due to a death in the family. Still,

AMPUTATION

I chose to stay.

I was able to spend some time with the host of the conference, who I learned had been suicidal years prior. After sharing my story, he asked me, "Have you forgiven yourself?"

I'm not speechless very often, but I stuttered, "Uh … maybe a work in progress."

He said, "It's as simple as looking in the mirror and saying, 'Alicia, I forgive you.'"

Ultimately, I left that conference with the question weighing heavily on me: "Will you settle, or will you maximize your God-given potential?"

I headed further east in anticipation of a few days on the beach. It took me two hours to open the visor mirror and speak those words out loud—"Alicia, I forgive you"—with tears rolling down my cheeks. The total drive was supposed to be three and a half hours, but eight hours passed before I finally found a room that night. I felt like God weighed me down with yet another question: *Will you trust me with the details when you don't know the destination?*

This trip led to working with Brad, a branding professional I had met at the conference, sitting on my porch two weeks later. In the fall, my real estate brokerage received its license and I was on a mission to reach out to a thousand homeowners facing foreclosure by year-end with a handwritten letter offering empathy, options, and hope. I recruited some help and the mission was accomplished.

Then came January, post-mission, post-holidays, post–Alicia's five-month adrenaline rush for the new business. I bottomed out. I felt like a bomb had been dropped on my world with no warning whatsoever. I had been doing so well. *What the heck? Why now? Why am I struggling to breathe again?* Hello, grief. I remembered that my counselor had told me, "The only way beyond grief is through it."

I had been distracted and high on several self-help tactics, from working out to daily cold showers, for a year, not missing a beat. Here is what I learned: Self-help helps, until it doesn't. I'm not suggesting that anything I was doing was bad. In fact, they were all good and beneficial things. They just weren't enough to bridge the gap between what I thought my life would be and what my reality was. Self-help doesn't resolve grief. The only way beyond grief is through it.

AMPUTATION

SELF-HELP HELPS, UNTIL IT DOESN'T.

It was time to ask for help, yet again, and that doesn't come easy for an independent gal raised with the sentiment, *Where there's a will, there's a way.* Mind you, this is a sentiment I believe with my whole heart. However, you gotta have the will before you can find your way, and that was a growing feat with each passing day.

If you can't do anything else, muster up the strength to ask for help, because as Pastor Jud Wilhite says, "It's hard to heal what you will not reveal."

CHAPTER 8

THE LEGEND

I was sitting at the six-foot foldable table in my dining room across from Lauren and Kristen, two gals from church whom I invited over to do a book study called *Find Your People*, by Bible teacher Jennie Allen. My sister had started a group in Kentucky the year prior, and I was encouraged by the community she created. I've never really had close girlfriends, and to my dismay, guy friends weren't shaking out very well for the long haul. The fact that I had invited two women to my house outside of my family was a miracle.

I blurted out, "We are turnin' a leaf tonight!"

They looked at me, alarmed.

"I don't think I've ever had just women over for dinner!"

MORE THAN A SECRET

We all laughed, and they cheered like most females who I never hung out with do. We dove into the taco soup and dialed up my most heroic friend, Tonya, on Zoom. Although I'd known of Tonya for years through extended family, when I headed to the beach after the Raleigh conference that summer, I reached out and we met in Cape Charles, Virginia. Although our paths had crossed at family celebrations on a few occasions, we had never connected one-on-one, but I always thought she would be a cool person to get to know. Not your average Joe, Tonya spent thirty-one years serving our country in the United States Navy—a *hero* by definition. I have the utmost respect and gratitude for anyone who serves our country, and Tonya was no exception. I was forever indebted and forever grateful before we even met that day.

Mind you, outside of my family, I did not have any close female friends—at least not the ride-or-die type—but I was hungry for connection and community. I stepped outside of my comfort zone and reached out. At that first one-on-one meeting with Tonya, what was intended to be lunch turned into a six-hour conversation, starting over lunch, continuing at the bar, and concluding at the beach as the waves crashed against the boulders.

THE LEGEND

I had never felt so safe with another female outside of my family in my life. I told her everything, including the details of my recent affair. She was full of empathy, grace, and compassion. We shared, we laughed, we cried, and, most importantly, we embarked on a friendship that few may ever understand or experience.

It's important to know, I've always gravitated toward men. If there's a room full of people, you will likely find me engaged with the guys. I learned in my first stretch of counseling that men are task-oriented and tend to connect on tactical levels like work, weather, sports, and politics. Women tend to connect on an emotional level by sharing how they feel. No wonder I've always been a guys' gal. Emotions? Feelings? What are those and who on God's green earth wants to talk about them?

I was so out of touch with my feelings when I started counseling that Jane had to dumb it down to various emoticons. I had a sheet of paper with a happy face, sad face, angry face, laughing face—you get the picture.

"How do you feel?" she would ask.

"I don't know," I would respond.

Jane would direct me to my cheat sheet to answer the question. Then, she got really audacious and asked me to start my journal every day with "I feel . . ." Eventually I graduated from using the pre-K emoticons and now defer to a wheel of emotions to help me identify what I'm feeling.

Here is what I learned: God gave us feelings and emotions to inform us, not to lead us. They are there to keep us safe. They don't always tell us the truth. As Annie F. Downs says, "Feelings can ride but they cannot drive!" I still journal how I feel and five things I'm grateful for every single day. It's not magic, and it doesn't take away the pain or resolve the grief, but I've found these practices to be healthy and help me come to grips with my current reality. Being honest is the first step to healing. Every. Single. Time.

I was sharing over dinner with my women's group that I felt like I needed to get back in counseling but wasn't sure where to look or who to reach out to. My first counselor, Jane, had retired. Both women lit up and immediately thought I would connect well with one of the executive pastors at the church who had recently opened a non-profit counseling center in honor of her late brother, Josh. The legend's name was Rachel Long, founder and president of Joshua Center.

THE LEGEND

The next day, I stepped away from the bar to take her call.

"Yes, thank you for your quick response," I told her.

"I look forward to meeting you tomorrow," she replied.

On the first night, I walked into a strip mall–style office building, shook Rachel Long's hand, and turned left into the room clearly set up for little tikes but good enough for adults alike. Before me was a small round table, office chair on each side, a comfy cloth-lined chair, and a small couch. She also had pictures hanging on the wall above the cubbies where the kids' "grief boxes" rested. Smiles and love poured off the wall, conveying memories of loved ones and their littles, some of whom were no longer here. It was sad and joyful. These kids had experienced loss no child should bear and yet were being loved and supported with their pain right where they were. "Two things can be true," I recollected.

The opposite wall had four canvas-like images with words representing the stages of grief. It didn't make sense to me. I don't remember much about our first session beyond sharing my story and Rachel asking the question, "Is it possible that Mav was the father figure you never had?"

Silence.

To be clear, I have the hardest-working, most patient, loving, willing, and able dad a girl could ever ask for. I would not be where I am today without his workaholic genes! He's a likable guy with a passive personality, would rather follow suit than create a stir, often turning to humor to avoid discomfort. I inherited his quick wit and seasoned sarcasm, but by the grace of God, I missed out on the humor! My dad never crossed me, never called me out; rather, he did his best to guide me in peace or dodge the conflict altogether.

Mav, on the other hand, was just like me. He didn't invite conflict, but he wasn't scared of it either. He had a dominant personality, was extremely confident, bold, and courageous. He was a privately sarcastic, self-described mix of Daniel Boone and John Wayne with Lynyrd Skynyrd as his heroes, although the Eagles were predominant in his speakers along with the Sirius radio channel "70s on 7." When he was distracted, I'd flip it to the Garth Channel, where I'd mostly recognize the songs from their initial release, not something from before my time!

Mav was a risk-taker, a thrill-seeker of sorts, who respected me *and* crossed me often. Sometimes, I'd swear

THE LEGEND

he would pick a fight just so we'd have to make up. He knew the buttons to push, how hard to push, and when to push them. I couldn't kill him for loving him, but there were times I sure wanted to.

Mav had a softer side, too, not lacking in contentious humor. I can recall him asking one night after I had alluded to the fact that I wanted to honor God with my life and body, "You think there's any chance he's asleep right now?" Lord, have mercy.

I could tell Rachel was on to something, perhaps yet another tentacle complicating and confusing my healing. She had my attention, and curiosity was lurking. I had already learned that anything we try to move on from without feeling, we are damned to repeat. What we don't walk out we will act out. I had unintentionally emotionally checked out for a few months while on mission impossible, reaching out to homeowners facing foreclosure, and now my emotions were all-consuming. Mav came back into town from winter training earlier than any year prior, and it was eating me alive.

I unloaded on Rachel: "I have begged him to tell his wife about the affair, get all the cards out on the table. Then each of us could evaluate and navigate life from there. He doesn't want to risk losing what he has worked his whole life for. Despite him saying he doesn't care, I feel like his image and how people will perceive him influences how he handles our situation as well. He fears losing his kids and grandkids, who I've always championed his relationship with. I even tried to spoil them as much as I could when they came to town. I understand, I wouldn't want to risk losing my niece either, but it was seemingly impossible for us to acknowledge it just isn't going to work and respectfully let go.

"If he hadn't been telling me he was working to resolve 'the situation,' that he loved me and wanted to spend the rest of his life with me for the last two years, post-affair, three years since I spent every possible waking hour working with him, maybe I wouldn't feel like a ball of confusion wrapped in pain. He wanted to resolve it amicably, and so he has pacified and justified his way through each day, each decision, each commitment, or lack thereof, at my expense. He's never been number two, nor will he ever be, because he would never tolerate the side effects. Therefore, he will never understand or comprehend what it is like.

"You might wonder, why didn't I call bullshit and run a hundred miles per hour in the other direction the

THE LEGEND

first time he ditched me in the name of saving face? The same reason I mentioned earlier. I have always wondered why so many women remain with men who are physically abusive; it's always seemed so ridiculous to me. With four billion men on the planet, why don't you go find one that treats you with dignity and respect and makes you his number one priority? Why didn't I run instead of engaging in a four-year affair until I literally reached the point of feeling so much pain from being ditched, degraded, abandoned, and belittled that I wanted to die? I can remember sitting on my bedroom floor, holding my knees to my chest, quivering, screaming, bawling, telling God I'm not selfish enough to take my own life but He could take it for me.

"Here is what I could never get past: *The pain of remaining in an affair as number two with a man I had fallen deeply in love with was unbearable. The pain of ending an affair with a man I had fallen deeply in love with was unbearable.*

"I tried to end it by my own willpower and strength for over a year, always surrendering to the desires of my flesh to be loved when we had the opportunity to make love. I've asked God to sever the soul ties, take away my desire, and yet, to say I struggle to let go is an understatement.

"I feel guilty for ending everything, Rachel. I was his person; he told me things that not even his own wife knows, things that hurt him and still hurt him. This strong, tough, prideful cowboy melted behind closed doors with me."

Just then my memory fled to a time when he had written me a letter to convey how he felt, which I communicated to Rachel. "He came in somber one night after dark, kicked his boots off at the door like normal, and stood with his back to my kitchen sink, letter in hand. I was sitting on a bar stool about ten feet away, fighting my own emotion as I saw his emotion, before he even began."

That triggered another memory. Mav was sitting on the last bar stool, closest to the end of my peninsula. I was standing across from him about three feet away, my hands in his, leaning over the bar. We were both a hot mess. He said, "I've shed enough tears to fill a lake. I'm telling you, I've never cried so much in my life. My family hasn't even seen me cry but maybe two times in my whole life."

It seemed to rattle him, the fact that he was so torn up, over me, over us, over this situation, and he didn't

THE LEGEND

know how to fix it, any of it. He looked down, noting the difference in the skin on our hands and the age difference it represented.

"Look at that," he said, "we might have ten years of fun at best, and then what, you still want to go and do, and I'm so old I just want to stay home and grow so jealous that I force you to stay home so nobody else steals you away. How is this supposed to work?"

I immediately replied, "I don't care about our age difference. It's just a number. We will make the best of the time we have, and I will forever be yours and only yours if you choose to resolve your situation."

I told Rachel, "He fought for me harder than anyone ever has. He trusted me more than he trusted anyone on this earth. I was the closest friend and confidant he'd ever had. He still trusts me, and that weighs on me in light of telling Mary, because I don't want to negate his trust; that would only create more guilt. I feel guilty because I know he is lonely, and I am too.

"I feel guilty for not respecting his wife. I feel guilty for living a lie with her.

"There's a constant conflict. Some moments I miss him so much, and it's all I can do to get control of my thoughts, not let the good memories and feelings negate my critical thinking. Other times, I feel so somber and sad toward Mary. Sometimes I feel both on the same day, even random triggers of each feeling in the same moment. Two things can be true."

It was only our second session when I said, "I guess I'm just reaping what I sowed."

"Whoa! Whoa! Whoa!" Rachel gasped. She said that this scripture is a caution *and* an encouragement! There is instruction, reproof, and *encouragement*. Jesus Christ went to the cross so we don't get what we deserve! That is the character of Christ. I reap what I sow, and I am sowing good seeds.

I can't even begin to tell you how many times I remarked, "She made her bed, now she gets to lie in it," as I was growing up. Rachel responded with a hint of disgust, "Somebody's gotta teach you how to get out of bed and make it."

Rachel explained that empathy is the marriage of grace and mercy. Empathy says, "I see you. I choose you and understand to the best of my ability what you're going through and I'm not going to punish you." I realized over several sessions that I had never really experienced female

THE LEGEND

empathy. I wasn't trained with it. I struggled when an acquaintance or friend would voice any seemingly negative thought about Mav whatsoever. I would respond, "Anything you say about him you must say about me." I learned in time that those comments from others were votes for me, not attacks on him. Empathy.

Rachel challenged me to stop beating the crap out of teenage Alicia, reminiscing on a time I had rebelled in my youth. Rather, she wanted me to give that girl empathy as I felt my way through it. And oh, how imperative it was for me to feel my way through it—all of it. Rachel made it clear that if I didn't, delayed grief would keep resurfacing. Unprocessed grief can turn into a lot of things, she advised, mistrust and suspicion being some of the most common. She encouraged me to make decisions for child me, teenage me—and to say I struggled is an understatement. She recognized this block in my brain and reframed it for me in such a way that opened the airwaves.

"How would you treat your niece if it were her broken heart?" Rachel inquired.

Without missing a beat, I said, "I would tell her I love her. Jesus loves her. We are both crazy about her and only want what is best for her. I would tell her it's gonna hurt bad, real bad, and it's okay to cry, it's okay to be angry, it's okay to be sad. I would tell her that I settled in the past and it cost me many years, tears, and heartache, money and time spent getting help and healing. I know the pain seems unbearable at the thought of goodbye, but not as costly as missing what God has for you. I would hug her, kiss her forehead, and hold her as long as she wanted to be held. I would send her cards and flowers and chocolate and horse stuff every single day until the pain was no more with that boy. I would affirm her and share God's promises with her until I was blue in the face. I would call her, text her, and go see her a lot! I would surprise her and take her on trips to discover God's beauty everywhere. I would tell her that the loss probably has much sweeter fruit in it than the win in life—look for the honey in the rock."

Rachel gave me permission to hurt over him, no matter what the relationship was based in. She said my values and ethics don't relate to the sorrow I feel. "Do you ever feel like Jesus has condemned you for your pain, ethical or not? Has Jesus ever retracted empathy because it was unethical? Jesus ran to the repentant and walked with them in their pain," she reminded me.

THE LEGEND

Perhaps unethical sorrow? I realized I couldn't control the sorrow. It's a divorce, death, and first-love loss. It's a catastrophe. I was hurting like hell and growing spiritually, just like Paul. As I often say, two things can be true at the same time. Joy and pain are not exclusive.

"It takes a lot of courage to stop a relationship you really want, and do it on your own terms," she reminded me often. "It takes a strong woman to walk away from an emotionally weak man."

> # JOY AND PAIN ARE NOT EXCLUSIVE.

"I'm over two years post-affair and still a train wreck. People say, 'Don't look back; focus on the positive and your future.' Unfortunately, I don't have to look back because he's in my windshield nearly every time I leave my house, which makes the latter a pretty tall task," I remarked.

Rachel encouraged me to start recording triggers, anything and everything that elicited a reaction of any kind. Over the next several weeks I wrote down everything, from seeing a load of hay, to hearing someone order unsweet tea, to seeing Mav standing outside as I drove by, to that Kum & Go gas station—you name it, I saw triggers everywhere.

This is fantastic, I thought, *now I have a long list to remind me of what triggers me.* I came with my ever-growing list and was challenged to come up with a replacement for each and every one. For the record, therapy is not for the faint of heart.

Some were easier than others. Instead of early morning coffee from Mav, I had coffee with Jesus as I read, studied, and journaled. Very, very different. One satisfied the flesh, the other was healing my soul, and yet both involved early morning, medium roast, McCafe black coffee.

I thought about waking up to the sound of Mav's boots coming across my porch before the sun rose. *There will be those sounds again, with a man who worships the ground I walk on,* I told myself. When I passed Mav on the road, I would say, "He's not for me," even though everything in me wanted him to be.

Rachel said I had to create new pathways in my brain, and the language I used was imperative in the

THE LEGEND

training. I was making painful progress, changing my thoughts, and my heart was going with it, she told me, though ever so slowly. It hurts, it breaks, it bleeds, and I have to release.

When Easter rolled around, I made the neighbors a pie when I would have ordinarily made Mav his favorite homemade coconut cream pie. I had always found great comfort and peace in the gentleness of his kiss on my forehead. Now I give my nieces and nephew that gift of calm and comfort every chance I get.

At one point, I was sitting with the two local girls from my book study group in a Starbucks parking lot after being run out at closing time. I was telling them about identifying triggers and replacements. I proceeded to tell them the story of the Kum & Go gas station and how seeing that gas station or name is a trigger.

My former campus pastor quickly remarked, "Well, we should take a road trip and get some hot dogs and a Coke from the Kum & Go so you will have a new memory!"

I grinned and said, "I was thinking I need to get married and go have sex in the Kum & Go parking lot!"

I'm surprised there wasn't a fatal crash on I-65 that night, as loud as they screamed in shock. They came from the straight and narrow; I did too.

That same night when they asked what was hard right now, I said, "The lack of physical touch—that's my number one love language."

Sincerely, one asked, "Would a hug from a friend help?"

Without missing a beat, I asked, "Would you rather masturbate or have sex? No, a hug will not help!"

"Don't worry, I'm never hugging you again," she said, laughing.

My other church friend turned red as usual and said, "I can't with you, I just can't!" —laughing, of course.

Although I'm able to find or create humor in some triggers and replacements, it is painful and healing work. I didn't realize at the time how imperative it was to find someone who could and would hold space for the totality of my loss. This whole unraveling has clearly revealed itself as a marathon, not a sprint, and having a trusted soul with the capacity to walk through it with me has been priceless. After all, Jesus said to the adulteress woman, "Go and sin no more," not, "Go and sorrow no more."

I was reminded of the shirt my sister gave me that read, "You can't throw stones while washing feet."

CHAPTER 9

COURAGE TO HEAL

*"If you don't heal from what hurt you,
you'll bleed on people who never cut you."*

—Unknown Author

THE HEARTSTRINGS FELT like steel cables that were beyond my ability to cut. I had learned to live without my physical connection to Mav, despite it being the greatest connection I had ever known. However, I could not in any way, shape, or form bear the thought of losing him entirely, of losing my person altogether. There was an emotional, physical, and professional bond to release. Perhaps I was making strides physically and professionally two and a half years after the affair, but our emotional connection was the one to be reckoned with. It was going to take a fight that I could not possibly prepare my heart, mind, or body for.

When I would think about Mary, all the Sallys in the world (which is the name I had given to all the women in my predicament) who I would one day serve with this story, and Jesus, I was done. My *why* was growing. When I selfishly thought about Alicia or Mav, I wanted it to be. But I couldn't have Mav without interfering with Mary, Sally, and Jesus, or the example I set for my niece and now nephew. So I had to be done. There was no other option. The song "Would If I Could" nails the way I felt, especially the lines "I would if I could, but I can't, so I won't, but I want to."[2]

How do you choose not to love someone you love? I would ponder. *Can I love something and not have it in my life the way I used to? Why hasn't God taken my feelings away? Why hasn't God severed the soul ties? How can something so wrong feel so right? Will my heart and mind ever align? How do I let someone I know and love become somebody I used to know? Me without him?* The love we had for each other was a curse in these circumstances.

He could have his life while loving and befriending me in secret, but if I loved him, my life stopped. The mental and emotional connection we shared was one to be reckoned with.

HOW DO YOU CHOOSE NOT TO LOVE SOMEONE YOU LOVE?

Despite seeing Mary, or at least her vehicle, almost daily, I still couldn't bear the thought of potentially hurting Mav. I could count on one hand the number of times I had gone on a date since ending the affair, always sure to meet somewhere that there wasn't the slightest chance of Mav showing up. Although never spoken, I think we both knew I wouldn't engage in another serious relationship as long as he was near.

I had often communicated with Mav how hard it was to see him with his wife, especially upon reciprocating I love you. So he was very intentional to fly solo as much as possible when he wasn't with me. By now, though, nearly three years post-affair, he had Mary as his copilot again.

He would say, "Well, she was here when you and I met; that's different than you going out and finding someone else." Of course it is.

I don't believe he wanted to hurt me either, but like he always said, "Somebody is going to get hurt."

He wasn't out to hurt his wife; he loved her "as the mother of his kids," he would say—*and* he loved me. He told me I was the best he ever had, the greatest person he had ever known. I sincerely feel like he would have loved nothing more than to show me off to the world as his. One day while dreaming about what it would be like to live together in the light, he commented, "I'd feel like the king of the mountain."

He had a death grip on my heart and soul. Was it lust? What man, just in it for sex, is still holding on to a woman nearly three years after she stopped the sex?

Rachel suggested that I work on releasing Mav as the gold standard. *This man that took me to the moon and showed me all the stars, the man who I've laughed and cried with, screamed and pleaded with, you want me to demote him? Cakewalk.*

He was the best I've ever had by a long shot. In fact, I'm concerned whether I will ever experience this depth of connection again, let alone a stronger one. Will I ever find a man to match or beat him? Aside from a few minor details like being married, he seemed perfect for me.

"You're too wonderful to be his secret." I could hear my first counselor's voice. I used to consistently feel degraded, belittled, and abandoned as a secret mistress. Now I felt broken, vulnerable, *and* empowered with purpose. I was starting to see how God might take what the enemy intended for evil and turn it for good. I felt a steady reassurance that there would be purpose in this deep and relentless pain as I moved toward serving the woman I used to be.

You are fearfully and wonderfully made, I recollected from Scripture. "Human rejection can't change that," Rachel stated.

I shared with Mav that I couldn't recall a time before this I had ever been rejected in my life. It made his blood boil.

"I did *not* reject you," he insisted.

"Not choosing me, regardless of the cost, is rejecting me," I stated in a calm and firm tone. It was like sending him an invitation to fight. Truth hurts.

At this point, despite all the words, songs, and

messages continuing to indicate his care, concern, and love for me beyond just friends, I knew he couldn't do this. He couldn't leave. He wouldn't leave. He didn't have it in him.

CHAPTER 10

FACING MY GIANTS

AFTER COMPLETING the mission I felt called to, getting the new real estate brokerage license that fall, and navigating the most painful and seemingly indefinite heartbreak of my life, I was contemplating what the next right step was.

I was sitting in on a weekly business coaching call when they issued the challenge "to be resourceful in terms of the people you know and the people they know that could benefit from your services." As I reflected and considered where I had spent the most time and made the most connections, the racetrack was the predominant place by far. So I reached out to the marketing office and was put into contact with a gal I knew. It had been a few years, but she was excited to see what we could put together. She sent me some options, and I asked if she had flexibility to create something outside of these. She said yes, and that's when the "winner's circle sponsorship" was born.

Mav and I were still trying to learn how to live in a new light while in an old place. Our communication had been minimal, short of a call from him in December about some horse papers one of his owners needed signed. The business part took about sixty seconds to discuss and then twenty minutes to catch up on a personal level until he had to go. I never received those papers.

Then early one morning in February, he sent me a text that stated, "Still waiting for the morning I wake up and don't have this big hole in my heart. All I can do is hope and pray that you don't have the same, since I wouldn't wish this on anyone. As always, every morning thinking of you."

I felt a wave of sadness and despair that I could not articulate. The only thing that flowed were tears. I later responded, "I am hurting too and am seeing a professional counselor again to help me work through this. These texts don't help my healing though; it's like pouring salt in a wound and brings many tears."

It was so hard to tell him that his text messages didn't help my healing, because reading them felt good in the moment. I felt wanted, cared for, and missed. It was a constant battle taking control of my thoughts, because a message like that would inspire daydreams about night things and how magical it would be to come together again after so much time apart.

I was honest with my counselor. I told Rachel everything, to the point that when she asked what was the one thing that would bring me relief and encouragement that week, I would give her a look of, *Are you kidding me?* She laughed, acknowledged how I felt, and gently reminded me that sleeping with Mav was not the way out of the wilderness.

I was working with the racetrack's marketing team and Brad, my branding guy, to nail down the sponsorship ads. Training was in motion at the track, but the racing season had not yet begun. This was a place I had spent an enormous amount of time, embracing a sport that reminded me what it was like to be part of a winning team, which inspired me to sustain the character of my horse barn as I converted it into an office and envisioned a winning team in real estate.

It was exciting to think about my company sponsoring the winner's circle, the very circle I had stood in time and again with Mav, Mary, and the team. It was also daunting to wonder how it would make Mav feel, seeing my name, my face, my number everywhere at his workplace. I really wanted to give him a heads-up. I wanted to consider him and protect him. My counselor discouraged the added engagement, saying this was a public space despite my considering it *his* space. The sponsorship was in place and signs were up for opening race day.

Crickets.

I thought for sure I would get some passive-aggressive communication. But nothing? It felt so confusing. As part of the sponsorship, we had a table in the clubhouse for Kentucky Derby Day, incorporating a local race card followed by a livestream of the Derby. My emotions were swarming, my mind was racing, my body was spazzing. It had been five years since I had been to a live race, let alone walked up to the paddock for the pre-race entrance and parade. This was a space that, little did I know, had grown to mean so much to Mav prior to my resignation from helping him with the horse operation altogether.

To say I was experiencing radical and out-of-character physical symptoms would be an understatement and too much information considering this isn't a medical journal. The only physical symptom that was familiar was another disc herniation. This time, my L4 and L5. My body was simply mirroring what my heart and mind were going through. The chart from the chiropractor's office five years prior flashed in my mind: "Mental and emotional stress are large contributors to physical health." Five years had passed, and here I was again, in complete distress over the same man and same situation.

Sure, the affair was over, and we were not working or doing life together, but I had never let go. It was clear he still longed for me as much as I still longed for him. Logic said it wouldn't work; it doesn't work. But we had continued to defy logic, holding on to some possible miracle that was threatening to kill me before it came to fruition.

Back then I typically saw Mav at the farm on race days prior to his departure to the track to make sure the guys and horses were ready for the races. I would leave the farm following chores, rush home to get cleaned up, and then head to the track. Mary typically went up to the apron while I hung out at the paddock and watched Mav walk up with the horse and groom from the barn. I would stand on the outside of the fence and watch the groom walk the horse around until it was time to put the saddle on. Mav stood at the corner of the assigned stall number, always in the backdrop.

When ordered to saddle up, the horse was led into the stall. If the horse was cool, calm, and collected, it would get saddled and go for another walk until the paddock judge ordered the jockeys to mount up. If the horse wasn't so calm, Mav and his assistant would saddle the horse in motion as the groom led it around the paddock.

I used to love watching Mav; his class and finesse stood out above all the rest. Little did I know until much later, he loved seeing me there too. After I quit going to races, he would comment on how he looked out from the paddock, up and down the fence line, eager to spot me, only to come up short. We never spoke when he was in the paddock, short of a quick text message if he needed something. At the time, it was the comfort of his being, and my being, in a consistent shared space.

My team and affiliates met in the clubhouse, a space I had entered for awards banquets, but I had never been there to watch the races. This felt different but not bad. I saw our beautifully carved aluminum sign that had been perfectly placed in front of the winner's circle. This was cool.

As the afternoon progressed, I knew my time was running out. There were two races left on the card. If I was going to face my giants, I had to leave the clubhouse. Any other day, I would have spent most of it outside. The day was stunningly beautiful with the sun shining and a gentle breeze. My heart raced. I had not spotted Mav at all from the second-story glass wall, presuming he was back in the barns waiting on his races. My group took the elevator down, and I limped out on the apron into the crowd of people. My leg felt numb, and my back was flipping out. *Mind over matter,* I screamed internally. *The only way beyond grief is through it. You can do this. You have to do this. Face your giants!*

I approached the paddock and there he was. It felt surreal. Mav stood in perfect form at the paddock entrance, looking forward, waiting on his horse. And nearby was none other than John-Boy, sitting in a relaxed state, waiting on the action to begin.

I snapped a picture. This was unreal, the two closest friends I've ever had, close enough to land in the same photo. One I had lost and the other I was losing. My heartbeat hurt. My mind raced with confusion, pain, and questions. I hoped nobody would try to engage in conversation at that paddock. Because if they did, I would have no recollection of who they were or what they said. I was not intoxicated; I was breaking into pieces inside while attempting to keep my composure outside.

I texted Rachel, my sister, and the core group of girls I had entrusted with my pain. My eyes were on Mav. I wanted to make eye contact. I wanted to acknowledge him in a very common public space for the first time in five years with respect and dignity. But it seemed like he was completely ignoring me. I could have sworn he had seen me in this crowd of people at that paddock fence. *This is unbelievable,* I thought. I considered sending him a text while my eyes were fixated on him. I could see it, him reaching down for his phone, reading it, looking up; he wouldn't be able to ignore me then.

FACING MY GIANTS

Instead, I waited. The horses were leaving the paddock headed out to the track for the pre-race parade. Everyone had turned to face the track, except me. I tried to turn ninety degrees so as not to look completely awkward, able to keep my eye on Mav while appearing to be interested in the upcoming race like everyone else.

Rather than head out of the paddock and down toward the apron, Mav walked closer to the fence separating the paddock from the sidewalk, which separated the paddock from the racetrack. He was looking intently at the horses on the track, standing sideways. I raised my hand awkwardly more than once.

Then it happened. He nodded. It was as if he were numb. John-Boy had disappeared to get into position for the starting gate. I walked with my group toward the apron to watch the race. Not even searching, I crossed paths with Mary and said hi. There were no warm fuzzy feelings by any means, but we spoke cordially, and I went on.

Mav and Mary's horse won that race. I stood there, twenty feet away from the entrance of the winner's circle, so happy for him and so very broken for me, for us, for what we lost when we crossed the line. It was the first time in the history of our knowing each other that I wasn't expected, let alone invited in, for the win picture. Grief is the gap between what you thought would be and what is. I grieved.

One of my associates and I hung around for the last race and then sat at a tall table by our sign. We were right in front of the winner's circle as everyone vacated the premises. I was anticipating Mav and Mary would walk by to get their golf cart and head back to the barn. My associate asked if I was okay. I don't really remember what I said. I saw Mav and Mary, an owner, and a few others standing in a circle format. I remember wondering, *Where do I fit in the picture?*

They disappeared. I had no idea where they went because I was confident their golf cart was still down by the paddock. Maybe they went inside the casino to eat. *How could he do that after a night like tonight, seeing me at this place for the first time in five years?* I didn't know, but I knew it was time for me to go.

My three-mile drive felt like an eternity. I limped into my house and lost it. I mean *lost it*, collapsing to my knees, bawling my eyes out, screaming at or to God, probably both. It felt like someone was reaching two sets of claws into the center of my chest cavity and slowly pulling them apart to make sure I felt the pain of every shift in motion and every ricochet thereafter. I thought about the women I had been feeling called to reach through this pain. I wondered if I would ever be able to articulate this pain, and so I recorded a video that could be seen if ever need be. I was on my knees, on my exercise mat, practically in a child's pose, trying to minimize the spasms in my back.

> # GRIEF IS THE GAP BETWEEN WHAT YOU THOUGHT WOULD BE AND WHAT IS.

I wasn't sure I would survive this pain. Could a person die from heartbreak? It wasn't the first time I had googled it and came up short. Was the mental and emotional distress going to cost me my physical life? I had openly talked about the pain I felt around Mav and this situation with my core group, but did they really grasp it? I texted the video of me in my most vulnerable and broken state to my core group that night. Perhaps this was the strongest thing I had ever done: let myself fall apart and invited other women in to witness it. Although alone, I didn't feel so alone the rest of that night.

"You cannot heal what you will not reveal." These gals knew about the affair. They knew I was hurting, but I always, always fight being emotionally vulnerable in front of others. Did they *really* know the depth of this pain? Did they *really* know the struggle? Did they have any idea how deep my wrestling was? Did they understand I was questioning if I would die from this loss? I've broken bones, sprained ankles, fought through mono, major disc herniations, sciatica—and all of it combined paled in comparison to the pain I felt losing Mav. I determined that night that my closest confidants and accountability partners needed to know and see the struggle, unfiltered.

Crickets.

This was eating me alive. I texted Mav. I asked him if he would be willing to talk a couple of days later.

He immediately responded. I conveyed to him I would prefer to meet in person but knew that would be a stretch.

He called. I didn't know what to say. I just wanted

to know we were okay and for him to know this whole thing was killing me.

He affirmed the same, said he started drinking after the races and hadn't been that drunk in years. He also said he was shocked when he saw me at the races, told me I looked beautiful, and that it was more than he could bear. He went into the casino and drank himself drunk. I recalled when I went back to the Opryland hotel and got wasted when I wanted nothing more than to numb myself after being challenged to not hold this secret anymore. I understood. I told him I went home and cried my heart and soul out that night.

He said he hadn't reached out about the sponsorship, although he had desperately wanted to, because he didn't think I wanted him to communicate with me. He had taken my earlier message as, "Don't text me," rather than as I intended, which was, "Please don't send heartfelt messages."

During all this, I was in constant communication with Rachel. She was continuing to learn the way I was wired and how helpful it was for me to know things were amicable between Mav and me as we navigated hard together, as we learned how to live in a new light while in an old place, especially when we saw each other on the road every single day. Dialectical behavior therapy (DBT)–informed pastoral grief counseling is what helped me navigate and survive this nightmare. Rachel has taught me that dialectical behavior therapy skills are the difference between someone telling me to calm down and someone showing me *how* to calm down. It is a skills-based modality and uses four modules to put *me* back in control of my emotions, instead of them controlling me.

It helped me regain control over my emotions and tame my thoughts. I felt an increased stability with my moods as we worked on anger, grief, lust, and abandonment issues. Rachel used "DBT-Informed Pastoral Interventions in Grief Counseling," which allowed us to meet outside of the four walls of the office, incorporate faith into my healing, and still use best practices. The pillars of DBT are strictly individual weekly therapy, participation in a DBT skills group, phone coaching between sessions to reinforce skills used in real-life situations, and a therapist meeting with the DBT consultation team weekly to discuss my treatment. Not all the pillars were appropriate for me, but some were and we used variations of it.

FACING MY GIANTS

I was learning how to create and build new brain pathways that reinforced new messages: "That's not for me" and "He's not for me." These became my unwanted anthem. It was truth, and while I didn't like this truth, I had to tell myself the truth *a lot* to prevent my feelings from running and ruining the rest of my life.

"It hurts, it breaks, it bleeds, release," I would repeat over and over and over. Feelings are meant to inform us; reason is meant to guide us. Someone who keeps breaking my heart is not in a place to care for my heart.

CHAPTER 11

THE FINAL GOODBYE

ONCE MARY LEFT town a few weeks later, Mav was able to come over and talk to me face-to-face. Like so many times before, he stepped in, kicked his boots off, but this time went straight to the peninsula in my kitchen and took a seat with a couple of beers in hand. He wasn't much of a drinker, just socially for work more than anything, and we used to share a drink or two leading into an intimate night. It helped us relax with all the tension that revolved around our situation. This night was different. We were post-affair. I opted for coffee, as I never reach for alcohol when I'm emotionally stressed.

MORE THAN A SECRET

Rachel helped me prepare and texted me throughout the evening. She knew I had detoxed enough to talk to him without sleeping with him. She knew I needed to make peace as far as it depended on me, tell him I forgive him, and tell him what I needed from him moving forward. Yes, I was living here first, but reality said we were both living here now, only separated by three miles and using the same service road every single day. I was like a recovering alcoholic choosing to live next to a bar. It was *brutal*.

My thought was, if Mav and I could come up with a congruent game plan on how to navigate this well, we would be okay individually and collectively. I wanted the same mutual respect we always had for each other privately to be exhibited in public when our paths crossed. I wanted to know he wasn't wrecking anyone else's world and that he was being loyal to Mary.

Three hours later I followed him out to his truck; two hours later, he left. We both got a lot off our chests. I worried, *What if that is the last time we ever have the opportunity to have a one-on-one conversation in person? What if this is the last time he ever comes over?* I didn't like the thought of either, but I felt tremendously better having had the conversation.

THE FINAL GOODBYE

The next day, a little before noon, I sent him a text that read, "Hey, thank you for processing with me last night. Please don't ever lose sight of my heart, always believe the best, and know I'll always be your biggest fan. Hoping and praying for the best for you and your family. We'll get through this." I also added a prayer and heart emoticon along with a quote that read, "Promise me. You won't forget our laughs. Our jokes. Our smiles. Our conversations. Our plans. Our tears. Our memories. Our experiences. Our friendship."

> **I WAS LIKE A RECOVERING ALCOHOLIC CHOOSING TO LIVE NEXT TO A BAR. IT WAS *BRUTAL*.**

He responded, "I will never lose sight of your heart unless it's through ignorance. I was dreading last night, but by midnight I was feeling so much better about all of it. I just want you to know from the bottom of my heart I am so sorry for the pain I have put yours through. Hope I am always your greatest friend and I hope the people involved with me learn to realize just how special you really are. And with a tear in my eye you will always be the greatest Person I ever met" (one tear drop emoticon).

I replied with gratitude and Chris Stapleton's song "Friendship."

We carried on with our individual lives, texting on occasion, and then I noticed two or three days had passed since I had seen him on the road. I was at my parents' home sitting on the back deck, waiting for dinner to get done on a beautiful summer night, as I peered out at that service road. It seemed very out of character and concerning that I hadn't seen him pass by in a few days.

I googled his name; the headline turned my stomach into knots, quickly driving away my appetite.

I shared the link with my core group and asked for prayers. I had no idea what was going on, no idea what they had accused him of, but my heart was broken for him, for them. I felt sad. I felt helpless. I felt like a secret who didn't have the freedom to reach out late at night to my friend, let alone show up. I knew Mav's world was

THE FINAL GOODBYE

spiraling right then and I wasn't with him. I wasn't there for him. All I could do was pray. It was torture, knowing he was just down the road. But so was Mary, and therefore, I couldn't be there to support him.

I sent a message the next morning: "My heart is so heavy this morning. I hate this for you guys. I'm a phone call away if you need an ear or a hand" (prayer and heart emoticon).

"Thanks, be in touch," he responded.

The days and nights were long. There were no updates online, and he was spinning in a million different directions, occasionally dropping me an update or a call. Through me, Mav bought some hay from my parents and that provided another justifiable reason to communicate.

He started voicing that he might sell the farm. I listened skeptically and asked him for the opportunity to help in any way I could if and when the time came—but not really believing it would. He is strong and has enormous grit. If anyone would pull through in a timely fashion, it was his team.

I recalled the words I had selfishly said to him so many times before: "You know, this is my hometown. You came here and stole my heart. Now you won't do anything about that. The least you could do is retire and go back home or anywhere but here!"

After nearly two weeks of not passing him on the road, I was retracting even that wish. I didn't want to do life without him here at all. *I hate this!* I thought to myself. *No, no, no, I would never wish any ill will on anyone, especially not Mav.* I never wanted anything bad to happen to him. I only wanted him to leave on his own will, out of respect, after failing to resolve our situation in such a way that freed us to live life together in the light. But now, now I was realizing that seeing him on the road was better than not seeing or hearing from him at all!

Something about him in this town and on that road had kept me feeling safe. Just his presence had become a source of comfort, and I had never realized it until now.

I thought back to our face-to-face conversation not even a month prior. The gratitude expressed for the good and encouragement he brought to my life, forgiveness for the pain and heartbreak, tears, smiles, and sarcasm. I was feeling all the feelings as I recollected asking him straight up that night, "Why didn't you let me go a few years ago instead of asking me to give you the winter to get your situation resolved?"

THE FINAL GOODBYE

Without hesitation, he asserted, "I thought we would be married by now."

To my dismay, Mav and Mary did indeed decide to sell the farm. Before we even got it listed, he received an offer. Upon negotiating the deal, I prepared the paperwork, coordinated the transaction for them, and saw it through to closing. It felt surreal. The very barn I helped complete and spent countless hours in over the years was now being conveyed to another outfit.

You may be wondering why I would be involved in the sale of their farm or why I would want to. Rachel helped me process this. For one, it gave me an element of control I had not previously had in this situation. I didn't get to choose the how, but I could help ensure a smooth execution, at least in this lane. I've spent my entire career in real estate, and in the public eye, Mav and I still had the utmost respect for each other. That would be very conflicting and perplexing to have anyone else represent them or facilitate the sale. Lastly, biblically, we are called to bless our enemies. Although I don't consider Mary an enemy, I got the impression from Mav that she despised me, but, as you may recall, he led her in decision-making and this was no exception.

I remember feeling so angry with God: "How could you let this happen? Why?"

Rachel helped me to see that God was answering our prayers, but I didn't get to choose the how. I hated it.

It was the morning of the closing, and I had to go by to meet the guys moving the storage container. I felt so defeated, fighting anger, tears, and emotion. I was disappointed and frustrated. Rachel and another friend from church would be staying with me that night, and so I had prepared for goodbye and had massive support in line following Mav's departure.

Then I learned that both Mav *and* Mary were on their way, which meant we would not have the opportunity to say goodbye. Mav had previously assured me that if she came up for the closing, he would come back to tell me bye. Surprisingly, he came to my office for the closing alone, but she was three miles away anticipating his quick return.

"Why didn't she just come to the closing?" I asked him.

"She's not going to embarrass herself. She's not going to put her jealously and insecurity on the table for everyone to see."

THE FINAL GOODBYE

After the closing, Mav stepped outside and was talking with one of the buyers. The other buyers left the office and headed to the farm. Mary was already calling him wanting to know where he was, not realizing one of the buyers hadn't arrived back at the farm yet either. It had been four and a half years since I was intricately involved in their lives and yet the suspicion and jealousy were still all-consuming for her.

It sucked. I was pretty emotionless that night. Mav got home that night and was on the road again hauling horses solo the next day, as I recall. We talked on the phone more that weekend than we had talked in months. He affirmed what he had been telling me in recent weeks and months, how much he still cared for me, that I was crazy if I thought he loved me any less than he did before, and how if we could fall off the side of the earth and be together where it wouldn't affect anyone else, he would spend the rest of his life with me.

The next day, Mav was headed back home. We were on another call, and he told me one of his kids asked him to take Mary on a trip that week, the same week he was supposed to be returning to the farm. I voiced my dismay and even had tears that night on the phone. It felt so fraudulent. Here he was telling me he wanted to be with me but was considering taking a vacation with his wife? Likely to his surprise, I realized it was their anniversary week and made mention of it.

He tried to play it off: "Oh, I bet that is why my kids are suggesting it." He said he had no intention of going; he was just sharing with me.

Early the next evening, I got a text: "Please don't get mad. My daughter asked me to please take them down there. Just real hard to tell you and real hard to tell her no. Thanks for understanding."

I lost it. I mean batshit crazy lost it. I fired off twenty-nine text messages in less than two hours, plus called liberally. Even though we had not been physically intimate in three years, it would be a lie for either of us to say we didn't love each other and still longed to be together. The thought of him completely dismissing my plea not to go, not to magnify the lie, not to celebrate an anniversary that wouldn't even exist if she had been open to amicably separating, not to be a fraud, sent me spiraling.

He was bringing out the worst in me once again. I didn't flip any tables or put any holes in the wall, because I didn't want to have to fix them, but don't think I didn't

THE FINAL GOODBYE

want to. I felt rage like I had never felt before, a side of me that I didn't know existed until this man.

Like flipping a switch, I remembered something was different this time. I had a counselor. I had her personal cell number. *Call Rachel,* I thought.

After venting and calming down with Rachel, we came up with a plan and wrote him a text: "I just got off the phone with my counselor. I'm not going to call you or text you. If you decide to uphold your promise and create space and time to meet with me, let me know."

"Thank you," he replied.

Five days later, he was on his way back, this time flying solo. I had spent the week processing and preparing with Rachel once again. He pulled in behind my former barn, now office, got his pup situated, and came in the door behind me. I had been pressure-washing some concrete and the storage container that we had moved from the farm he just sold to my place. We had not spoken since his sudden vacation, and I was certainly feeling tense.

I told him that the choice he made to magnify the lie he was living, to intentionally and deliberately choose something he knew would hurt me when the opposite decision would not have hurt anyone—perhaps only created some disappointment—was the straw that broke the camel's back. I shared that I believed the love we have for each other is a curse under these circumstances. He can have his life and love me, but if I love him, my life stops. I've suffered pain to get to this place in my healing journey, and I'm not going back. I told him that I didn't want to go through it anymore. It's not fair to him and not fair to me. I told him I'm committed to finding the Alicia he so desperately wanted back, the Alicia he met nearly a decade prior who was alive and well, full of life, speed, vigor, and "a little bit of crazy," in his words.

It wasn't an uninterrupted meeting. He had to leave about an hour in to take care of some business and tried not to come back because it had been a tense discussion. But ultimately, he did come back, this time sitting on the plastic picnic table on the patio behind the office. I remembered Rachel telling me that I had control of how it ended.

I was sitting across from him and asked him to take his sunglasses off. I could sense the emotion. He half shook his head and respected my request. I reached out

THE FINAL GOODBYE

across the table for his hands. Hand in hand, I told him I loved him and that I suspected I always would. I told him I forgave him for the hurt and the pain that he had caused. He started crying. I told him I didn't want to live like this anymore, and he said he understood. I also told him I didn't want to say goodbye, but I must because he could love me and still live his life, but when I love him, my life stays on hold, even eight years later. We were both adults and must find our way now, and it hurts like hell. We agreed that if there were any major turn of events in our lives or with the people we love, there was an open door to reach out. I cried the whole time. He was crying and said he had to go.

We both stood up and embraced, soaked in tears and fear and pain.

He stuttered, "How appropriate; this is where it all started, and this is where it all ends."

He walked toward his truck. I stood frozen, bawling as quietly as I could. He had the rear driver's side door open, putting his pup back in her cage. I began walking in that direction as all I could see were his boots fixed on the ground. He was feeding her and giving her water.

"Does she need some fresh water?" I asked.

"No," he replied under his breath. "Okay, one more hug?"

We cried. He got in the driver's seat. I was standing between the door and him like so many times before, but this time was the last time. And it felt unbearable.

He was quivering and started rubbing his chest profusely. "Are you okay?" I asked.

"No, I have to go."

With tears running freely down both our faces, I stepped back and he closed the door as he pulled away with the same four-horse trailer he embraced me in for the very first time. I raised my hand in the air as if saying "Goodbye, see you soon," not knowing if I would ever see him on this side of heaven again.

Once I caught my breath and felt my heartbeat again, I texted Rachel: "He just left. To say that was the hardest goodbye of my life is an understatement."

Later, I said, "It feels like a double-edged sword. I don't want it to end, and I don't want to live on hold the rest of my life. I don't know what I'm supposed to feel about this, but I don't feel good about this right now."

Rachel responded, "You are enduring a lot right now. It will not be this painful. You are making choices for future you; it will not always hurt this bad. Alicia, I am with you; the level of strength and heartache you are feeling has to be exhausting. You did it. You did it. I'm just in awe of you."

A couple of hours later he sent a text wanting to leave me with Whitney Houston's song "I Will Always Love You."

I cried and responded, "I know you will and you know I will. I wish you nothing but the best. I love you and I release you," adding a broken heart emoticon along with Reba's song "Just Like Them Horses."

The guilt, internal battles, temptation to reach out, mental war zone, and even sexual hauntings (for lack of a better term) that ensued in the days, weeks, and months to come were nothing short of exhausting and depressing. The unraveling of the ties was atrocious. Rachel reminded me often that one of the key factors in my healing was being honest. I could tell her anything and everything, and I did. I held nothing back, especially when I was on the verge of reaching out to him. I reached out to Rachel instead.

She said, "It is fresh, and you deeply loved him. It will take a bit. You must fully process something to fully release it."

I was thankful and found comfort in our amicable goodbye, the same type of amicability he had longed for with Mary in order to resolve their situation. I could not imagine carrying on with life at odds with him. I continued seeing Rachel on a regular basis as I navigated the grief and all its terrible side effects. I was doing my best to acknowledge how I felt each day while choosing to put my best foot forward.

The day after Christmas, I received an unexpected text message: "I heard congratulations are at hand. I know how much your nieces and nephew mean to you. Hope you made it through the hustle and bustle of the holidays. I'm sure all the neighbors are a little heavier thanks to your generosity. Lol [laughing emoticon] Don't know about you but I'm still waiting for that one morning. I hope reaching out is okay—always thinking of you."

I had just become an aunt for the third time and apparently Mary had seen the post on Facebook while they were traveling on Christmas day.

I offered appreciation and continued, "I'm not sure you will ever know or understand the toll it has taken and continues to take on my heart and soul. I fight to show up

THE FINAL GOODBYE

and layer in escapes for when the grief hits. I know you aren't for me; you chose otherwise and yet I've never experienced pain like this in my life. I can only hope you don't put another heart on the line and that someday I will be able to live and breathe again."

This one outreach sparked consistent and ongoing communication with a few hundred miles between us. I learned that his trouble at work had all been resolved completely in his favor. They had nothing on him, which was great news.

He recalled that an old piece of farm equipment he inherited from his dad was still in the woods at the farm he sold, and so I reached out to the new owner and went to pick it up. Upon letting him know through a text, in perfect fashion, he said, "I wonder about you sometimes. Thanks a bunch."

I enjoyed our text message conversations and occasional phone calls—a dose of false comfort, I suppose. However, I did not enjoy being limited by whomever he was with or who was around, because he was choosing to keep me a secret. It didn't take long for tensions to rise and our normal fighting over how to navigate the situation to ensue.

I concluded a Tuesday text thread with, "I give up. I just named several things earlier that you intentionally did despite my heart cry to do otherwise. So yeah, you can help by not ignoring my heart cry, by not throwing me in the ditch when it's not convenient for you. But we both know you can say all the right things and have the best of intentions, but you know as well as I do if it comes down to saving face, looking out for someone else or being there for me, you're going to save face and I'm gonna see the ditch."

One moment we were okay, the next we were trying not to kill each other through a phone. It was a comfortable toxic, an acceptable known hell. We both knew the song and dance all too well.

Still, I was shocked by the text I received the very next morning. I remember thinking, *Something has happened, and I don't know what.* My mind was racing. I tried to call, but he wouldn't pick up, even after I asked him for the respect of a conversation. He texted back that he could when he got back to the house where Mary was.

What, so you can flat-out lie to her with me on the phone? I wondered.

In the text, he told me to "never contact him again for the sake of his marriage." He said he had promised

THE FINAL GOODBYE

Mary he would cut off all contact with me and that he wasn't going to break that promise—*despite all the lies he's told and massive lie he has continued to live*, I thought.

This man, who had drilled into my head, "Don't ever burn a bridge; you never know when you'll need to cross it," just burnt the bridge between us. I felt so confused. This man, who for so long had fought with his wife for me like no human ever has, just threw me in the ditch for Mary to witness almost a decade later.

Rachel, call Rachel.

My blood rushed while Rachel listened.

Part of me wanted to call Mav from a different number. Part of me wanted to have my dad, who now knew about our affair, call him. Part of me wanted to call Mary.

"Will tomorrow Alicia be pleased with that decision?" Rachel asked.

"What the hell, Rachel. Who asks a question like that when bombs are exploding?"

None of the options racing through my head gave me peace. I was in a frenzy. But I had been taught my whole life not to react but to respond. As much as I hated it, I chose to do and say nothing further that day.

MORE THAN A SECRET

Rachel and I scheduled an emergency session and there we came up with a game plan. I would formulate a text message that I would send to both Mav and Mary in a shared thread at my next session six days away. I met with a couple of my core gals Wednesday morning at the church. We walked and talked, went to lunch, and killed time all afternoon until my session.

As the time got closer, my nerves fired up. How would Mav respond? How would Mary respond? *Would* they respond?

I've always felt like it was Mav's place to tell her about the affair. But when he took a stand against me, I felt like that opened the door for me to take a stand for *truth*. My text, pre-typed in my notes app and reviewed by my inner circle, read, "I've taken a few days to process and seek counsel. Mav, it felt very deceptive, contradicting, and completely out of character for you to send the texts you sent. I have always spoken with the utmost respect for you guys publicly on the rare occasion I have run into a mutual connection. Anything to the contrary is false. Mary, please feel free to come to me directly with questions from the past or present. I will tell/show you the whole truth if you want to know the truth. Nothing

THE FINAL GOODBYE

means more to me than my integrity. You can rest assured; I will no longer have any direct contact with Mav."

Rachel asked if I was ready.

"Ready as I'll ever be," I replied.

I knew this man so well, inside out and upside down. His messages to me did not come from his heart; this was fear. I copied and pasted the message into the text thread, my hands shaking, my heart racing, my body quivering. I wanted the cards on the table so bad I couldn't see straight. I wanted the truth—*all* of it—out. I didn't want to be a secret, and I didn't want to hold his secret any longer.

Mav replied in the group thread, "We appreciate you reaching back out. There is no hard feelings. Texts are very cold to begin with, and so we hope we did not come across harshly. You of all people know all the gossip and bullshit that goes on and it just gets pretty tiresome. The whole deal results from me eras[ing] text [messages] something I should not have done. This was not about bringing hardship towards you and we wish you the best."

"Bullshit!" I exclaimed to Rachel.

"He just gaslighted you," Rachel said.

I didn't even know what that meant. I went from

being anxious to angry in a split second. I sat with Rachel for over two hours, processing, anticipating a text response from Mary.

Crickets.

Do I respond? Part of me just wanted to call bullshit. Part of me wanted to ask when he was picking up the farm equipment. Part of me wanted to call a spade a spade and tell Mary the *whole* truth in that text thread right then, right there.

"Is tomorrow Alicia at peace with that?"

Damn it, Rachel, I thought.

I chose not to respond, thinking that I might in the days to come.

The next night I was working late in the office, and my dad had swung by and left. I was headed out shortly thereafter. I tied up a few loose ends, killed the lights, locked the door, and got in my truck to head up to the house, which is only a few hundred feet away. As I pulled out from behind the barn, I could see lights coming from the road approximately 1,400 feet down the drive. About halfway between the office and the road there is a fork in the drive; I would make a hard right turn to go to my house or continue straight all the way out to the county road.

THE FINAL GOODBYE

These lights were coming fast. My heart started racing, my palms sweaty, adrenaline rushing. It was a sports car with tinted windows, flying in here like they owned the place. *Mary's hired a hit man*, I thought. *My house will be a death trap.* I suddenly saw *Walker, Texas Ranger* flash in my mind: Walker would charge the enemy, swerve to the right into the grass just before the crash, missing the trees, duck to miss the bullet, fire shots, and fishtail back onto the drive.

So I did just that—well, except I didn't have any shots to fire.

I flew out of the drive and took a right on the county road, had my dad on the phone to get his gun and head back my way. I slowed down on the road so I would know if said hit man pulled out of my drive or just blew up my office.

"Hurry up, where are you?" I asked emphatically.

My parents' home was only a half mile away but it seemed like ten miles at the time. When I finally passed my dad, while on the phone, I told him, "Yes, that car. Catch him, and be careful!"

I drove the block. I worried that whoever was driving the sports car might have dropped someone off to hide out behind my office, waiting for me to return. I called one of my associates, asking, "Do we have an Amazon order coming tonight?"

"No, it says 10 a.m. tomorrow," she replied.

"Great, I'll update you later." *If I'm not dead*, I thought to myself.

Dad and I were on and off the phone every minute it seemed. I suppose it's hard to hold a phone, hold a gun, and chase a hit man down a county road.

Dad called and said, "I lost him. He was flying."

"Okay, meet me back at the office. I'm going in to check the cameras. Call me when you get there. I'm locking myself in," I said.

I was pulling back in the drive, cautiously looking for anything out of character. I saw something with a reflection near the door to the old tack room. I pulled behind the barn/office, which was lit up like a Friday night football field. I backed myself to the door, while unarmed, got in, and locked the door behind me.

Dad arrived. I let him in, thankful he was armed, and then locked the door again. I started watching the security video playback. There it was, sports car, tinted windows—and out stepped a man in a blue vest with

THE FINAL GOODBYE

reflective stripes. I ran to the tack room door, opened it, and sure as you know, there was the Amazon package, which had arrived twelve hours early in an unmarked car. I laughed in relief, which beats crying every time!

I tried to imagine what I would have told my mechanic if I had wrecked my truck in the forty-year-old pine trees in my own yard. "Oh, I was just practicing my *Walker, Texas Ranger* moves on a perceived hit man, also known as the Amazon delivery man!"

I wonder what that delivery man thought!

Later, I was sharing the story and reflecting on the text I had sent to Mav and Mary. One friend replied, "I can't believe she didn't reach out to you. If that was my husband, I don't care if we were in the same truck, I would have speed-dialed you for truth on speaker phone! She doesn't want to know; she doesn't want me or the world to know. But she knows."

I kept wondering, Would he attempt to call me from an unknown number? Would he go get a Straight Talk phone like he'd done before he got his own phone plan that I knew was now back on the family plan? Would he do anything? Would he even attempt to inform me about what happened that triggered these desperate actions to save face?

I told him months ago at our amicable goodbye that I was planning to write a book. He looked at me like I had lost my mind.

I said, "I will change your name, but I am not letting this pain be wasted."

He did not comment. Why would he let the story end this way? How could he? I wished he had never reached back out to me after our amicable goodbye four months prior. Though it was the hardest goodbye in my life, at least it left me at peace with him.

But to cut me off with no explanation, no conversation, based on hearsay and some deleted text messages, after falling in love and holding on with a death grip for years—after everything he'd told me, everything he'd shown me, *this was it*?

Jane, my first counselor, came to mind: "You don't have to understand everything." Mav and I had always said no matter what happened, neither of us wanted to end up hating each other, ever. *So, how could he do this like this?* As Lainey Wilson brilliantly sings, "even the devil don't go there."[3]

Why did it take him cutting me off in such a cold and heartless manner to fully let go?

THE FINAL GOODBYE

My heart still hurts, and deep down I don't doubt I will always love that man, but this I now know: *We will never be again.*

As a secret, being ditched, belittled, and degraded was par for the course, but only between me and him. Nobody else ever knew in those moments that I got shafted. I always protected him. By involving Mary, this time it was different. Although I took it for years in private, I realized I had to take a stand for truth and protect myself moving forward.

I had longed for an amicable goodbye. I had control of how that ended, and so it ended in peace, love, and tears. I didn't get to choose how this time, and it kills me that it ended with disregard, disrespect, and massive deception. He operated out of fear rather than love, and that was devastating for all of us.

Perhaps I got what I needed, not what I wanted.

CHAPTER 12

POST-WAR

THIS PICTURE-PERFECT portrait that most people have painted of me, by walking out from behind the bush, because of grace, unashamed—they will now see a wounded, free, and perhaps more beautiful version of me.

There is a necklace made by Cary O'Keefe that stole my heart the second I saw it in Fort Worth, Texas. It is called Target Practice and it consists of a triangular piece of fine silver, bullet riddled, with the bullet drop hanging on the end of the chain. How is it possible that this piece is even more beautiful after being obliterated? From the smooth piercing to the tattered edges, it hangs from my neck, giving me hope that God will indeed use my story for his glory, that what the enemy intended for evil, God will use for good, that you and I may actually be more beautiful *with* our pain and scars than without.

It has been through the forging and breaking that I have learned true humility and empathy. Despite knowing right from wrong, you never fully know what someone has gone through or is going through that makes them vulnerable and weak against the enemy's ploy to steal, kill, and destroy. Sin can look shiny, attractive, stimulating, and be remarkably fun—until it's not. First Corinthians 10:12 says, "If you think you are standing strong, be careful, for you, too, may fall into the same sin" (NLT).

I never, ever thought I would participate in such a destructive action that had the potential to hurt so many people and have me knocking on death's door. I was arrogant and never saw the need for accountability in my life, because I thought I was stronger than any temptation that crossed my path.

I would love nothing more than to sit kneecap to kneecap with Mary, own my part in this affair, apologize, seek her forgiveness, and encourage her healing. I took someone who wasn't mine, and for that I will always be remorseful. As far as how it relates to Mav, Mary and I both got screwed. He lied to and led each

POST-WAR

of us on a road leading to nothing short of pain and heartbreak. He had his cake and got to eat it, too, for a season. It sounds so cold and heartless, requiring extraordinary strength for me to even acknowledge it, let alone type it, because I don't believe it was ever his intent. The truth is, nobody won.

I don't hate him. He's not a bad guy. Mav made some really bad decisions, as did I. I hate the way he navigated the situation, especially the ultimate and permanent termination. It was deceptive, fraudulent, and abrupt. I had said for years that I trusted him with everything but my heart, and he ultimately proved that to be true.

I wanted all the cards on the table and in the light of day. I wanted to know that Mary knew the truth—all of it—and not for my own benefit. Mav and I will never be together again, regardless of his marital status. But I wanted Mary to know the whole truth because healing *always* starts with truth. We could all truly begin a complete healing journey, including Mav, if he would admit the truth. But you cannot heal what you will not reveal. And, as of this writing, over a year since that final group text, Mary has not reached out to me for the truth.

Some may crave justice for Mary, and to that I would say, there is justice. Her kids and grandkids are hers and Mav's together, and the man I had an affair with is the same man she is married to and has spent decades with. She has known and loved the same imperfect, passive-aggressive man as I did. I would also say that in the pain I walked through to navigate this situation, I have paid and continue to pay consequences far beyond what I could have ever imagined, and rightfully so.

I'm a broken and vulnerable vessel today, completely surrendered to Jesus and fully accountable to a core group of women in my life, who have the freedom to ask me anything, anytime. I proactively tell Rachel *everything*: the raw and unfiltered truth of every nightmare, sexual haunting, trigger, desire, imagined fear, uninvited imagery, pain, feeling, and hang-up around this situation. I hold *nothing* back, because I want to fully heal, and I know that in every instance, healing begins with truth.

I have lived what Wynonna Judd sings: "When you hit rock bottom, you've got two ways to go, straight up or sideways."[4] I am empowered with purpose and have space for nothing but healing. I am stronger for being broken. I am more resilient and growing in endurance. I'm not

POST-WAR

afraid to admit my mistakes and am willing to put in the heart-wrenching, soul-crushing, physically exhausting work of walking through grief and healing from the trauma of my affair in order to fulfill the call I feel God has placed on my life: *to serve the woman I used to be.*

God knew this would be part of my story, and I believe with all my heart, someone else will be better for it. Romans 8:28 gives me confidence: "And we know that in all things God works for the good of those who love him, who have been called according to his purpose" (NIV). I will forever regret the sin of adultery and the immorality of my decision to participate in an extramarital affair. I regret the pain I have caused and the hearts I broke.

To say that I fully regret this whole story would be a lie. If it hadn't been for Mav, and the awakening I experienced as a result of knowing him and loving him, I'm not sure I would have ever known anything more than coexisting with my former husband as "roommates." I certainly would not be writing this story of hope and inspiration for women across the globe, desperate for a lifeline. I believe Romans 8:28 with my whole heart.

I'll be the first to tell you, it didn't always *feel* like God's goodness was following me despite the affirmative in Psalm 23:6: "Surely your goodness and love will follow me all the days of my life, and I will dwell in the house of the LORD forever" (NIV). More often than not, I felt like I was being punished for being obedient upon ending the affair. Is it possible that the pain I felt was a sign of progress? Perhaps there is a different standard for measuring God's goodness.

God encouraged the people of Israel in Joel 2:25 when he told them, "I will restore to you the years that the swarming locust has eaten" (ESV). God's promises for restoration and abundance after hardship, even self-inflicted hardship, are *not* dead! I have found that Jesus is gracious and compassionate, slow to anger and abounding in love.

Never in a million years would I have dreamed of writing a book about my sin in hopes of inspiring others to dodge it, end it, and heal from it. I saw my legacy revolving around real estate, living a debt-free life, and/or pouring into the next generation. But serving women, being vulnerable, connecting on an emotional level, letting tears fall for others to see? Funny, God.

God gave me this life with a guidebook and free will. That guidebook, the Bible, is full of wisdom and direction on how to live an abundant life in a world where He tells us we will have trouble. Our Creator, the very God who knit us together in our mothers' wombs, knows something about what is good for us and what is not, what will help us and what will hurt us. The parameters He provides are for our protection, not our punishment. He loves us more than anything in this world, so much so that he sent his only Son to die for us, to bear the burden of our sin so that we may live forgiven and free and, by grace, unashamed.

You are accepted and loved unconditionally.

It's impossible to chase Jesus and live in sin. I chose to follow my way for a few years, and it ended in the greatest pain and hardest goodbye I've ever experienced. Will you turn from your sin and fall into your heavenly Father's arms where forgiveness and freedom wait? It's not the words, it's the posture of your heart that matters. If you are ready, take these words and make them your own.

> *Heavenly Father, I believe in you, and I love you. I am so sorry for the sins I have committed and the way I have lived my life. Please forgive me. My life is yours from this day forward. I receive you, Jesus, as my Savior and my Lord. I surrender myself to you, to your will and your*

way. Thank you for your grace. Please give me hope and strength as I learn to walk with you through this valley. Amen.

Proverbs 28:13 says, "People who cover over their sins will not prosper. But if they confess and forsake them, they will receive mercy" (NLT).

Girl, God is strong enough to carry what is crushing you.

Second Corinthians 4:8–9 says, "We are hard pressed on every side, but not crushed; perplexed, but not in despair; persecuted, but not abandoned; struck down, but not destroyed" (NIV).

I'm committed to living the rest of my life God's way, praying daily, *Not my will, but thy will*, regardless of the cost. I choose not to be a secret any longer, for God's Word says, "I am fearfully and wonderfully made" (Psalm 139:14, NIV). I also continue to find comfort in Genesis 50:20: "As for you, you meant evil against me, but God meant it for good, to bring it about that many people should be kept alive, as they are today" (ESV).

Girl, I see you, with a broken soul, always trying to hide your pain, tears, and swollen eyes from your closest friends, family, and coworkers. It's exhausting, I know. Do future you a favor and find yourself a trusted soul, a therapist, to let it all out, someone who won't judge or condemn you for your pain or decide when the pain should end. Find someone who will show up, listen, and care, someone who has the capacity to walk through this with you for the totality of it, to the finish line and beyond—even for the comeback.

> # GIRL, GOD IS STRONG ENOUGH TO CARRY WHAT IS CRUSHING YOU.

I've heard it said that someone's hardest season often surfaces their greatest and most meaningful purpose. It rings true for me. My greatest pain, my hardest goodbye, inspired me to write this book, to serve the woman I used to be. It is my hope that this book finds every woman who is desperately searching for someone to relate to, someone who has been in her shoes, to draw hope and inspiration from. I pray she would muster up the courage to break free from the toxicity and trauma of an extramarital affair and, most importantly, find Jesus with open arms, clothed in mercy, grace, and forgiveness. My ultimate hope and prayer is for this book to be the resource I couldn't find when I reached the point of no return.

Telling a trusted soul the truth is the only way out. It breaks the unforgiving and evil bond of the secret that holds you back from the forgiveness, freedom, and grace that await.

It is what it is, and it will become what you make it.
It was never supposed to be this way, girl.
You are worth *more than a secret*.
Would you like to get well?
Go heal.

> "Behold, I am doing a new thing; now it
> springs forth, do you not perceive it?
> I will make a way in the wilderness
> and rivers in the desert."
> (Isaiah 43:19, ESV)

APPENDIX

POEMS AND REFLECTIONS

Do You Even Know?

Your last-ditch effort to save your face
became my saving grace.
Truth be known, with tears in our eyes,
every attempt at prior goodbyes
was only a desperate hope for an intermission
that would open the door for succession.
Do you even know the grip you had on my soul?
The lock on this cage?
Do you even know everyone I told,
wondered if it were so?
You appealed to her, you appealed to me.

MORE THAN A SECRET

You lied to her, you lied to me.
She had your money, I did not.
The kids, the grandkids, it makes no difference.
It's all a lie you live, and they live with,
unbeknownst to them.
You can change, receive Jesus's saving grace,
or burn in hell over a lie I live to tell.
It rattles my soul, don't you even know?
The man upstairs, his forgiveness and freedom await.
Please phone home, cowboy, make it right.
I wanna see you on the other side
in the beaming light.

POEMS AND REFLECTIONS

Love Goin' Nowhere . . .

Electric from ten feet away.
Enough to lead anyone astray.
The work, the laughs, the tears,
It all seemed so sincere.
Six months in, before our love affair.
First sign of jealousy, where do we go from here?
You said we would be okay,
there would be a divorce before it would go there.
The louder she screamed, the harder she fought,
the tighter your grip on this young heart.
I felt so safe, so wanted, so thirsty
from the fire burning inside us
and growing between us.

You touched my leg one summer day,
lit me up with your embrace.
If that's all that happens, "it was fun," you said,
"take a few days to think about it."
What is there to think about?
I was ready to flirt with my desire,
play with fire.

The flames burned bright walking into the fire.
Sensation so strong, it didn't even feel wrong.

MORE THAN A SECRET

It was a dream, except for every goodbye.
Would I get a morning rendezvous,
afternoon delight, or almost all night?

Four years later, the burn,
the pain from living in vain.
To die would be gain.
No less care, no less fire, no less desire.
We never wanted goodbye.
I wanted to be by his side.

POEMS AND REFLECTIONS

Never Thought I'd Be That Girl

Straight and narrow was the only path I'd known.
Nothing would make me more angry
in this world than lies of my own.

Never thought I'd be that girl.
My roots ran deep in God, Garth, and Strait.
Grew up in a world where right was right
and wrong was wrong
if you wanted heaven to be home.

Full of life, speed, and drive,
he said you're just a little bit crazy.
I was born a fighter,
I don't know lazy,
nothing dare stand in my way.
A man twice my age
matched my way,
a force to be reckoned with.
Who dare get in our way?

MORE THAN A SECRET

Never thought I'd be that girl.
My roots ran deep in God, Garth, and Strait.
Grew up in a world where right was right
and wrong was wrong
if you wanted heaven to be home.

You're married, I'm married,
we can't do this,
my conscience said that day.
And just like that, the fruit of another lured me away.
I'd never had so much fun,
living life in the fast lane,
until death seemed more appealing
than living life this way.

After all, it was God's protective grace
to give us the straight and narrow way.
Thank you, Jesus, for teaching me this way.
May I bleed your forgiveness, grace, and compassion
for the rest of my days.

POEMS AND REFLECTIONS

More Than a Secret

Girl, you are fearfully and wonderfully made.
God said it was that way.
No man can take that away.
If he ain't walking with you in the light of day,
you better put them feelings away.

My parents didn't get it all right,
but they sure raised me right.
I am worthy, I am loved, humble, and kind.
I have self-respect, dignity, and pride.
Why did I turn a blind eye?

When you're not the only one,
he must look out for number one.
Ditched, belittled, degraded,
abandoned, and rejected
were all in the number two gun.
It will take a toll on any soul.
I'm a secret nobody knows.

MORE THAN A SECRET

Will I remain a secret or heal?
It's hard to heal what I will not reveal.
It hurts, it breaks, it bleeds.
I gotta release for my niece.
She deserves only the best version of me,
living free.

"The only way beyond grief is through it,"
my first counselor said to me.
"What you don't walk out, you will act out"
and "if you don't feel your way through it,
you will be damned to repeat it,"
my second counselor said to me.
What I thought would be is not this version of me.
It's time to make a change,
not only for me and my niece,
but in order to serve the woman I used to be.

POEMS AND REFLECTIONS

Stones

Let he who has not sinned cast the first stone.
Jesus said go and sin no more.
Has Jesus ever condemned you for your pain?
Self-inflicted or a victim,
to Him it makes no difference.

Jesus ran to the repentant,
walked with them in their pain.
It was never in vain.
"Unethical sorrow" some may say.
Values and ethics don't correlate
to the sorrow I can't control.
Jesus never said go and sorrow no more.

Has Jesus ever retracted empathy from the repentant?
Find yourself a trusted soul,
someone who won't judge you or condemn you
for the toll on your soul.

Do they have space for the totality of it?
It's a marathon, not a sprint.
Ask rather than assume and stop at nothing
until you find one soon.

MORE THAN A SECRET

Someone who will show up, listen, and care,
never tiring of your tears.
Grief is a beast, with no way to prepare.
Find yourself a trusted soul when healing is the goal.

POEMS AND REFLECTIONS

How?

How do you do what you do?

The grip on this heart,

the tension in this chest.

Where is the air in this breath?

The memories, the good ones,

what do you do with them?

Half a grin to the left, a tear down the right.

The subtle reminders of the joy we shared.

The jolt of rejection screaming reality.

A whiplash—mind, body, and soul.

Not a day goes by I don't think of you.

What will it be today?

A sweet memory, a flat tire,

teary eyes, or swollen face?

How do you do what you do?

MORE THAN A SECRET

Lonely Alone

Lonely alone in my own home,
silence sings an unwanted song.
I'm not made to do life alone.
Better alone than in the toxic zone.

Lying single in my double bed,
thinking of you in your bed.
Your back turned toward her,
thinking of me crying myself to sleep.

It's hard doing life with her wishing with me.
At least you have company.
I know it weighed you down
watching me drown.
It hurts. I don't doubt any amount.
Just not enough, I would say, to your dismay.

You are young, beautiful, and smart.
You can do anything, you would say.
How do I do lonely alone in my own home?

POEMS AND REFLECTIONS

The Man I Knew

The man I knew
the world has never known.
Forced to grow up too fast,
the jock of his class.
He'd cowboy up to prove he was a man.
Hard as steel, cold as ice,
he'd learn to make nice only for the ladies in his life.
A will to win, a force to be reckoned with.

Stubborn as me, he stood his ground.
A tin man wrapped in cowboy attire,
never showing his heart, hurt, or desire.
Damn a cowboy down.
He'd never shed a tear with anyone near.
Always something to prove.
But when he came in and let me in,
I saw the toughest man in that room.
That's when I knew we were in tune.

Living life in the fast lane, never feeling a thing,
what happens when you can't outrun pain?

*This book is not in lieu
of mental health counseling.*

Suicide Prevention: Call or Text 988

Domestic Abuse Hotline: 800-799-7233

Crisis Text Line: Text HOME to 741741

National Mental Health Hotline: 888-786-3092

Joshua Center: 317-698-1040 or joshuacenter.org

ABOUT THE AUTHOR

Alicia resides on a small farm, where she continues to walk out her personal grief journey and serve the woman she used to be. Alicia loves all things real estate and is honored to support Joshua Center in every way possible. She makes a point to visit her nieces and nephew across state lines several times a month in an attempt to be the aunt she's always dreamed of being! She holds on to hope for a God-honoring relationship in her future, with someone with whom she will share not only an unimaginable mental, emotional, and physical connection, but, most importantly, an unwavering spiritual connection.

A portion of all book sales will be donated to Joshua Center.

Stay Connected!

Website: www.aliciabarr.com

Email: team@aliciabarr.com

IG: @aliciabarrauthor

FB: aliciabarr

NOTES

1. "Once Upon a Lifetime," written by Frank Myers and Gary Baker, Concord Music, 1992, Album: American Pride.

2. "Would If I Could," by Dean Dillon and Skip Ewing, 1996.

3. "Devil Don't Go There," by Lainey Wilson, *Whirlwind*, BBR Music Group/BMG Nashville, 2024.

4. Wynonna Judd, vocalist, "Rock Bottom," by J.R. Cobb and Buddy Buie, *Tell Me Why*, Curb Records, 1994.

ACKNOWLEDGMENTS

First and foremost, to the Big Man upstairs—we have warred *a lot* over the last few years. I release the how to you and trust you will use my story, with all the broken pieces, for your glory. Jesus, thank you for loving me and never leaving me.

My first niece, "thank you" will never be enough. You are the reason I'm alive. From the news of your coming, to your arrival, to this beautiful life we share today—I love you more than life itself. You will forever be AA's Awesome Sauce!

My niece and nephew, you have added to my why to be the best version of me I can be. You are pure joy, full of life and love, with the best giggles in the world. I love you both to the moon and back!

Ashley, though the enemy nearly convinced me you

would do life without me just fine, I *cannot* imagine this life without you. You are my ride-or-die, the best sister I could have ever asked for, doing the greatest work on earth, raising the best nieces and nephew in the world to love Jesus.

Austin, thank you for loving my sister like Jesus does. Thank you for sharing the best babies in the world and championing our time together. Thank you for embracing me with grace, forgiveness, and love.

Mom and Dad, thank you for raising me right. Thank you for always showing up for me when I ask. Thank you for your unconditional love and support to chase God's call on my life, as crazy as it is!

My extended family, you know who you are and how you have shown up in my story. Thank you for your unconditional love, grace, and support on this beautiful journey called life.

Tonya, you closed a lifelong gap. I am forever grateful for you and the friendship we share! Thank you for showing up, listening to my heart cry, and offering unwavering support for my healing. I can't wait for our next adventure!

Rachel, I am forever indebted and forever grateful.

ACKNOWLEDGMENTS

Thank you for showing up. Every. Single. Time. You, my friend, are a legend.

My book coach, Ally Fallon. Thank you for your book *Write Your Story*, and for guiding me in the right direction right out of the gate! You threw the gut punch and heart hook all in one shot when you asked, "What about *More Than a Secret*?"

My publisher, Becky Nesbitt, you are a force to be reckoned with. Your energy, excitement, and grace for my story from that first call were contagious and invigorating. You are the sole reason I signed with Forefront Publishing. I trusted you before I even knew you. Thank you for your guidance and unwavering patience with me as an amateur author!

My editor, Mickey Maudlin, I didn't cuss you quite as much as I did Jesus, but I'm confident your ears were burning at times through the developmental edit! Thank you for warring it out with me, despite my ignorance with technology, to create the most impactful version of this story possible!

My senior editor, Jill Smith, and the rest of the Forefront team, each and every one of you played a pivotal role in getting this story to print. Thank you.

MORE THAN A SECRET

My branding guy, Brad Imburgia, founder of Ember Brand Co. Jill said it best: "I'm convinced that every author should have a Brad on their team." You are the *best*—thank you for taking this jump with me!

My publicity team, Storytold PR, thank you for taking me in under your wing without a name, without a following, without a clue. Ya'll ROCK!

My book marketer, Aryn Van Dyke with Book Rockstar, thank you for accepting the mission to get this book into the hands of every woman that wants it. I'm so thankful for your guidance and expertise!

Last but not least, to every character in this story, thank you for the role you played, good, bad, or indifferent. The world has a little more hope today.